D1455152

FUNCTIONAL EQUATIONS
IN
MATHEMATICAL OLYMPIADS

PROBLEMS AND SOLUTIONS
VOL. I (2017 - 2018)

BY

AMIR HOSSEIN PARVARDI

The University of British Columbia
Mathematics Department
Vancouver, Canada

MAY 2018

Dedicated to my lovely wife, Nadia.

Preface

Foreword by pco

To me, solving functional equations has always seemed similar to carrying out police investigations. Starting at the scene of the crime, we can immediately establish a certain number of properties (the values for certain configurations of variables, existence of cases in which simple properties can be used right away, etc.).

After collecting the initial clues and seeing how they fit together, we carry out a second search for properties, without necessarily immediately advancing toward a solution. We are content with widening the field of characteristics and information that we possess about the culprit.

Now comes the moment where the clues combine to grasp our attention (a profile of the criminal and similarities with known crimes start to emerge, etc.), and our field of suspects narrows. At this point, we only focus on the clues that seem to lead towards the emerging criminal profile. This continues right up until the discovery of the culprit.

In the world of functional equations, I add an additional step (and officially leave the world of police investigations): I look at the trail of clues that led me to the solution, and I simplify it, search for shorter paths, and essentially, *optimize* it. This step is intellectually satisfying as it produces solutions that seem *magical*, but it is not very satisfactory for a book like this one. It makes more sense, educationally speaking, to reveal the entire process, including the sterile reasoning branches (something many people ask me about when questioning my *motivations*).

My only regret in letting Amir Hossein use certain solutions of mine in this superb work of compilation, sorting and ranking, is that some of these solutions (whether they come from me or other contributors) remain a bit *magical* and not very educational. In this regard, it seems to me that the collection of reflections elaborated upon by the author throughout the first two chapters of this book must be read attentively. Often, these reflections motivate solutions proposed in subsequent chapters.

pco,[1]
May 29, 2018.

---

[1]Note from the author: thanks to Jenna Downey for translating pco's words from French to English.

About This Volume

Functional equations, which are a branch of algebraic problems used in mathematical competitions, appear in recent olympiads very frequently. The knowledge needed to solve olympiad-level functional equations is basically nothing more than a 20 page handout. Therefore, there are very few books on the subject in olympiad literature.

My initial goal for creating a problem set in functional equations was to publish a book of over 3000 questions solved by the user *pco* in the forum of High School Olympiads at AoPS Community. These questions were posted in the period [2003, 2018]. After starting the project, I soon realized 3000 is not a small number at all, and it is impossible to gather all those problems together (which would probably make a 3000 page book). Furthermore, nobody is willing to see three thousand functional equations. So, I decided to publish the best problems among these – as some were Crazy Invented Problems – which would be around 1500 questions. Also, I decided to publish these problems in a few lighter volumes instead of one thick book.

This volume contains 175 problems on functional equations, including those used in almost all latest mathematical olympiads (*2017 – 2018*) around the world. As mentioned above, most solutions were written by pco, but there were several other users who were kind enough to let me borrow their solutions and have it in the collection. Please follow the instructions for reading the book in order to get the best out of it.

Amir Hossein Parvardi,
May 28, 2018.

Acknowledgments

- I would never be able to finish this book without the never-ending support from my wife, Nadia Ghobadipasha.

- Most of the credit and respect goes to *pco*, as he was the man who motivated me with his hard work in solving algebra problems to create this problem set. Most of the solutions in this book are due to pco.

- The following is a list of people who gave me permission to include their solution in this book. The list is in alphabetical order. To respect their privacy, I'm just using the AoPS username of the author in case they did not want to reveal their name:

  - Catalin Dumitru (Buzau, Romania)
  - Evan Chen
  - Kevin Ren
  - Loppukilpailija
  - Minjae Kwon (Seoul, Korea)
  - Murad Aghazade
  - Navneel Singhal
  - Nikola Velov
  - Roman Buzuk (Belarus)
  - scrabbler94
  - Stefan Tudose
  - Sutanay Bhattacharya
  - talkon
  - ThE-dArK-lOrD
  - Tuzson Zoltán

- I am thankful to Pang-Cheng Wu and Ting-Wei Chao for giving me access to their notes on functional equations. I have used some parts of their solution for solving the general Cauchy's equation.

- Mohsen Katebi wrote Python codes which were used to generate an initial draft for the problems. His work saved me a lot of time.

- The cover of the book was designed by Ali Amiri. The photo in the background of the cover is the complex-valued graph of Riemann's zeta function and was taken from Meta.Numerics website.

- The foreword was initially written in French by pco. I am thankful to Jenna Downey for translating it to fluent English.

- Finally, thanks to Kave Eskandari, Reza Miraskarshahi, Abtin Eidivandi, Alireza Jamaloo, Koosha Irani, and Sohrab Mohtat, and Mohsen Navazani for their comments on the structure of the book.

Contents

Appendices

Chapter 1

Instruction for the Reader

1.1 How to Use This Book

1.1.1 The Preamble

This is a bank of questions on functional equations. So, you might want to skip the first parts and move to problem solving right away. But please don't. Take your precious time to read the next pages before trying the problems in the book. I can guarantee that no matter what your level is on the subject, you will find the content interesting.

1. Skim through definitions so we are on the same page. There are a few phrases which are frequently used throughout the text.

2. Do not let easy-looking titles in section 2.2 deceive you into thinking that the problems in that section are straight-forward and easy. Beside very basic definitions of concepts in functional equations, I give several examples in which those concepts are used, and a good number of the examples are not trivial at all. So, please do not skip reading this section.

3. In fact, section 2.2 gives you a gist of the solutions in chapter 4.

4. There are possibly concepts and definitions which need to be added to this preamble. If you feel that I should include an introduction to any specific topic, please let me know and I will add it in the next editions of this volume.

1.1.2 Problem Solving

After you read the preamble, you have 175 incredible problems ahead of you to solve! Some tips on how to solve them:

1. The problems have been separated based on the domain of the functions in the problem. Then each domain has its own special subcategories. Although problems on $\mathbb{R}$ are more popular in mathematical competitions, it is possible that you get a very hard problem over

$\mathbb{Q}$ or $\mathbb{N}$ in your olymiad exam paper. That being said, if it is the first time that you are solving problems from this book, I encourage you to solve one or two problem from each domain (rather than solving $\mathbb{R}$ completely first, and then $\mathbb{Q}$ and $\mathbb{Z}$). This way, you won't be focusing on one type of problem only.

2. Try changing the sub-categories of the problems that you solve periodically as well. For instance, solve two questions on existence-type problems over $\mathbb{R}$ (section 3.2.4) and then one on number theoretic functions (section 3.4.1), and so on.

3. Do not try CIP problems at home. CIP is an abbreviation used by pco. It is short for *Crazy Invented Problem*. Such problems were either randomly generated by curious students or are too hard for no good reason. There shouldn't be more than 10 such problems in this book, but I labeled them as CIP because they can waste your time if you are studying for an olympiad. These problems are difficult! So, even if you want to try them, do it at your own risk because they could each easily get two hours of your time and don't lead to anywhere.

1.1.3 Solutions and Hints

1. The solutions in this book were mostly written by user pco on AoPS. I have edited his solutions to fit in this book, but there are possibly errors in them. If you find any mistakes in the book, please send them to my email at `a.parvardi@gmail.com`.

2. Not all the problems have solutions or hints. There are a few ones that have neither a hint nor a solution, but I have tried to give at least a hint when the solution is not presented. If you want me to include your solution (and give you the credit) in this book, please shoot me an email.

3. In my opinion, the best way to solve problems from this book is to think on the problem for half an hour, and if you have struggles, check the hints. If there are multiple hints, do not read all of them at once. Read the first hint, try it, and if you still don't get the idea, read the next hint. The same is true for the solutions. Try to prove the claims made in the solutions before reading the given proof. This will improve your problem solving abilities.

4. Some of the proofs by pco (and other authors) are just incredibly amazing. Even if you solve the problem successfully, do not miss the solution if it is given in the book.

5. Enjoy!

1.2   General Knowledge on Functional Equations

This book starts with a chapter on basics of functional equations. I have tried to include almost all the necessary definitions needed to solve problems in the book. My approach is example-based so you can make a good connection to the problems and have a sense of what you are going to see throughout the book: you might know by a handful the whole sack.

For those of you who are enthusiast in reading more on the subject and learn advanced techniques in problem solving, I'm listing a few good sources that I know of:

- I never had the chance to read Venkatachala's book [1] as it is only available in Amazon India, but I have read very good reviews about it and it is considered as one of the best books on the elementary theory of functional equations.

- Chapter 2 of Small's book [2] contains detailed solutions to famous classical functional equations such as that of Cauchy, Jensen, and D'Alembert. Knowing a detailed proof for Cauchy's additive equation is a must for olympiad students, and hence this chapter is pretty much appreciated.

- Pang-Cheng Wu's recent notes on functional equations are perfect. I strongly suggest you read his impressive functional equations handout on AoPS if you want to learn cool techniques and see a bunch of amazing problems. I have used some parts of his work in section 2.3 of this book.

- Evan Chen's handout on functional equations is a top-notch work. Make sure that you read his notes. He also has a handout called Monsters on his website which is dedicated to difficult problems ("pathological functional equations").

1.3   Solving More Problems

If you cannot wait until I publish the next volumes of this book, keep yourself busy with solving problems from the following question banks:

- 116 Problems in Algebra by Mohammad Jafari has quiet good problems, especially in functional equations. Almost all the problems have been solved by AoPS members, and it is a good exercise for the reader to try those problems. Some of the problems are pretty tough (a few were used for Iran IMO team selection tests) and might be a good exercise if you are in for heavy-lifting.

- 100 Functional Equations by yours truly is a collection of problems posted on AoPS fora around 2009 to 2011.

- Functional Equations Marathon on AoPS used to be very active in good old days. Give its problems a try if you don't mind solving a few CIPs.

Bibliography

[1] Venkatachala, B. J. *Functional Equations Revised and Updated 2nd Edition*. Prism Books. 2012.

[2] Small, C. G. *Functional equations and how to solve them*. New York: Springer, 2007.

Chapter 2

Basic Concepts

In this chapter, we explore the basic concepts and definitions in the theory of functional equations. As an appetizer, let's start with notations.

2.1   Notation and Definition

- $\mathbb{C}$: the set of complex numbers.

- $\mathbb{R}$: the set of real numbers.

- $\mathbb{R}^{\geq 0}$: the set of non-negative real numbers.

- $\mathbb{R}^+$: the set of positive real numbers.

- $\mathbb{R}^-$: the set of negative real numbers.

- $\mathbb{Q}$: the set of rational numbers.

- $\mathbb{Q}^+$: the set of positive rational numbers.

- $\mathbb{Q}^{\geq 0}$: the set of non-negative rational numbers.

- $\mathbb{Z}$: the set of integers.

- $\mathbb{N}$: the set of positive integers. Also denoted by $\mathbb{Z}^+$.

- $\mathbb{N}_0$: defined as $\mathbb{N} \cup \{0\}$. Also denoted by $\mathbb{Z}^{\geq 0}$.

- $\gcd(a, b)$: the greatest common divisor of a and b. Also denoted by (a, b).

- $\operatorname{lcm}(a, b)$: the least common multiple of a and b. Also denoted by $[a, b]$.

- *WLOG*: Without Loss Of Generality.

- *RHS* and *LHS*: Right Hand Side and Left Hand Side.

- *Assertion*: an expression in a few variables. You constantly see phrases like

  "Let $P(x, y)$ be the assertion $f(x + y) = f(x) + f(y)$ for all $x, y \in \mathbb{R}$."

  This is because we don't want to write the equation $f(x+y) = f(x) + f(y)$ every time we want to plug in new values of x and y into the equation. For instance, instead of writing

> "By plugging in $x = 1$ and $y = 2$ into the equation $f(x + y) = f(x) + f(y)$, we find that..."

we write

> "Using $P(1, 2)$, we get..."

- *General solution*: a family of solutions to a functional equation which respects these two conditions:

  - Any function in the given form indeed is a solution, and
  - Any solution can be written in the given form.

Read more examples about this in section 2.3.3 of chapter 2.

2.2 Concepts

2.2.1 Injection, Surjection, and Bijection

If you are reading this sentence, you already know what a function is. So, I'm not going to define that. However, the definitions of an injective or surjective function might not be obvious for the reader. Instead of giving formal definitions, I would like to explain these concepts in examples.

- When we write $f : A \to B$ is a function, we mean that the domain of f is A and its codomain is B. The domain of f is the set of values that f can act on. For instance, if the domain of f is the interval $[1, 2]$, it means that $f(x)$ *is defined* for any $x \in [1, 2]$.

- The codomain of f, on the other hand, is a set that contains all the values that the output of f can get. Please stop here and read the last sentence again. With this definition, we do not require all elements in the codomain of f to be the image of some element in the domain of f. Let me give you an example to make this clear. Suppose that $f : [1, \infty) \to \mathbb{R}$ is given such that

$$f(x) = \frac{1}{x}, \quad \forall x \in [1, \infty). \tag{2.1}$$

Here, $\mathbb{R}$ is the codomain of f. However, there is no $x \in [1, \infty)$ for which $f(x) = 2$. In other words, there is an element in the codomain of f which is not *admitted* by any input.

- It now makes sense to define the set of all possible outputs of f. This set is called the *image* of f and is denoted (usually) by $\mathrm{Im}(f)$. In other words,

$$\mathrm{Im}(f) = \{f(x) : x \text{ is in the domain of } f\}.$$

For instance, in the example given in (2.1), the image of f is $(0, 1]$. This is because the reciprocal of a number $x > 1$ is always positive and < 1.

- So far, we have found out that the image of a function is not necessarily the same as its codomain.

- A very natural question that comes up here is the following: when is the codomain of f equal to $\mathrm{Im}(f)$? A function with this latter property is called a *surjection*, a *surjective* function, or sometimes an *onto* function. Consider the example in (2.1) again (assuming the codomain is $\mathbb{R}$). This function is not a surjection. However, if we set the codomain to be $(0,1]$, the discussion in the previous part implies that the new function is surjective. Formally, a function $f : A \to B$ is surjective if for any $b \in B$, there is some $a \in A$ such that $f(a) = b$.

- When talking about surjectivity, for any b in the codomain of f, we only care about the *existence* of an element a in the domain such that $f(a) = b$. If such an element exists, then the function is surjective. However, in order for the function to be *injective*, we want each element of the codomain of f to be mapped to by **at most** one element in the domain. That is, there should not exist any two different elements in the codomain which are mapped to by the same element in the domain. An injective function is sometimes called *one-to-one*. Formally, $f : A \to B$ is injective if and only if $f(a_1) = f(a_2)$ yields $a_1 = a_2$ for all $a_1, a_2 \in A$. The function $f : \mathbb{R} \to \mathbb{R}^{\geq 0}$ defined by $f(x) = x^2$ is surjective (why?) but not injective. The reason is that for any non-zero $x \in \mathbb{R}$, we have $f(x) = x^2 = (-x)^2 = f(-x)$ but $x \neq -x$.

- A function that is both injective and surjective is called a *bijective* function or a *bijection*. Some people tend to call a bijection a *one-to-one correspondence*, but not me. Can you think of a bijective function now?

Now, let's see an example of how we prove surjectivity or injectivity in a given functional equation. Consider first the following problem from Vietnam National Olympiad 2017:

Example 1. Let $f : \mathbb{R} \to \mathbb{R}$ be a function satisfying

$$f(xf(y) - f(x)) = 2f(x) + xy, \quad \forall x, y \in \mathbb{R}.$$

Call this assertion $P(x,y)$. We aim to prove that f is surjective. That is, we want to show that for any $b \in \mathbb{R}$, there exists some $a \in \mathbb{R}$ such that $f(a) = b$. Using $P(1,y)$, we arrive at the equation

$$f(f(y) - f(1)) = 2f(1) + y, \quad \forall y \in \mathbb{R}.$$

Consider $b \in \mathbb{R}$. Notice that the above equation holds for all real values of y. So, if we choose y so that $2f(1) + y = b$, or equivalently $y = b - 2f(1)$, we would have $f(a) = b$, where $a = f(y) - f(1) = f(b - 2f(1)) - f(1)$. This is exactly what we wanted to prove! Hence, f is surjective.

The following example is due to Dan Schwarz (mavropnevma), whom I truly miss.

Example 2. Given $f : \mathbb{R} \to \mathbb{R}$ that satisfies

$$\left(f(2^{x^3+x})\right)^2 - f(2^{2x}) \le 2$$

and

$$\left(f(2^{2x})\right)^3 - 3f(2^{x^3+x}) \ge 2$$

for all real x, we want to show that f is not injective. The point here is to look for reals x such that $2^{x^3+x} = 2^{2x}$. One can easily find by a simple search for such numbers that this happens for $x \in \{-1, 0, 1\}$. In fact, if we let $a = -1$, $b = 0$, and $c = 1$, then

$$u = 2^{a^3+a} = 2^{2a} = \frac{1}{4},$$
$$v = 2^{b^3+b} = 2^{2b} = 1,$$
$$w = 2^{c^3+c} = 2^{2c} = 4.$$

Therefore, for any $z \in \{u, v, w\}$, using the given inequalities in the problem, we find that

$$f(z)^2 - f(z) \le 2 \implies (f(z)+1)(f(z)-2) \le 0$$
$$\implies f(z) \in [-1, 2],$$
$$f(z)^3 - 3f(z) \ge 2 \implies (f(z)+1)^2 (f(z)-2) \ge 0$$
$$\implies f(z) \in \{-1\} \cup [2, \infty).$$

Since we want both $f(z) \in [-1, 2]$ and $f(z) \in \{-1\} \cup [2, \infty)$ to happen simultaneously, this means that $f(z) \in \{-1, 2\}$. Hence,

$$f\left(\frac{1}{4}\right), f(1), f(4) \in \{-1, 2\},$$

and so two of these values are equal to each other. This directly implies that f is not injective.

2.2.2 Monotone Functions

Definition 1 (Increasing Function). A function $f : A \to B$ is called *increasing* on an interval $I \subseteq A$ if for any $a_1, a_2 \in I$ with $a_1 > a_2$, we have $f(a_1) \ge f(a_2)$.

Consider the function $f : [1, \infty) \to \mathbb{R}$ defined by $f(x) = x^3 - x$. This function is increasing. Can you prove it? One way is to use the definition given above. The other way, which is much simpler, is to use calculus: $f'(x) > 0$ for all x in the domain.

Notice that if for all $a_1, a_2 \in I$ with $a_1 > a_2$, we have $f(a_1) > f(a_2)$, then the function is called *strictly increasing* (or *monotone increasing*) on I. Try to show that the function given in the example above ($f(x) = x^3 - x$, $x \in [1, \infty)$) is a strictly increasing function.

Definition 2 (Decreasing Function). A function $f : A \to B$ is called *decreasing* on an interval $I \subseteq A$ if for any $a_1, a_2 \in I$ with $a_1 > a_2$, we have $f(a_1) \leq f(a_2)$.

You should now be able to guess the definition of a strictly decreasing function. Sometimes people use the word *nonincreasing function* to emphasize that the function is decreasing, but not strictly decreasing. The same goes for nondecreasing functions.

Definition 3 (Monotone Function). A function is called *monotone* if it is either always increasing or always decreasing.

So far, the examples we have seen where functions with domain either $\mathbb{R}$ or $\mathbb{Q}$. Let's see an example of an *arithmetic function* now. An arithmetic function is any function with domain $\mathbb{N}$. That is, a function that acts on natural numbers $1, 2, 3, \dots$. We usually denote arithmetic functions with $f(n)$ (instead of $f(x)$) because naturally, n feels more like an integer. Note that arithmetic functions need not give integer values in their output. That is, the codomain of an arithmetic function is not necessarily $\mathbb{N}$. For instance, the function $f : \mathbb{N} \to \mathbb{Q}$ defined by $f(n) = 1/n$ for all naturals n is an arithmetic function, which is strictly decreasing (why?). Another example is $f : \mathbb{N} \to \mathbb{C}$, given by $f(n) = \log n$ for all $n \in \mathbb{N}$.

Example 3. An arithmetic function $f : \mathbb{N} \to \mathbb{Z}$ satisfies the following inequality for all positive integers n:

$$(f(n+1) - f(n))(f(n+1) + f(n) + 4) \leq 0.$$

We want to prove that f is not injective. First, notice that the expresion may be written as

$$(f(n+1) - f(n))(f(n+1) + f(n) + 4)$$
$$= (f(n+1))^2 - (f(n))^2 + 4(f(n+1) - f(n))$$
$$= \left((f(n+1))^2 + 4f(n+1)\right) - \left((f(n))^2 + 4f(n)\right)$$
$$= \left((f(n+1))^2 + 4f(n+1) + 4\right) - \left((f(n))^2 + 4f(n) + 4\right)$$
$$= (f(n+1) + 2)^2 - (f(n) + 2)^2 .$$

So, the given inequality becomes $(f(n+1) + 2)^2 - (f(n) + 2)^2 \leq 0$, or

$$(f(n+1) + 2)^2 \leq (f(n) + 2)^2 .$$

Define a new arithmetic function $g : \mathbb{N} \to \mathbb{N} \cup \{0\}$ by $g(n) = (f(n) + 2)^2$. Then, we get $g(n+1) \leq g(n)$ for all $n \in \mathbb{N}$. This means that the function g is decreasing. To see this, notice that if $a > b$, then

$$g(a) \leq g(a-1) \leq g(a-2) \leq \cdots \leq g(b+1) \leq g(b).$$

So, $g(a) \leq g(b)$ and g is a decreasing function. But since the output of g are non-negative integers (why?), the function g must be eventually a constant function because the smallest $g(n)$ can get is 1. So, let $g(n) = (f(n) + 2)^2 = c^2$ for all $n \geq n_0$, where c and n_0 are positive integers. This means that $f(n)$ can take only the values $-2 - c$ and $-2 + c$, and hence is not injective (see Example (2) for a reasoning).

2.2.3   Even and Odd Functions

Example 4. Consider the functional equation

$$f(xf(y) - y) + f(xy - x) + f(x + y) = 2xy,$$

where the domain and codomain of f are supposed to be $\mathbb{R}$. Let's call the latter assertion $P(x, y)$. Then, $P(0, 0)$ implies

$$f(0) + f(0) + f(0) = 0,$$

or simply $f(0) = 0$. Also, $P(x, 0)$ gives

$$f(-x) + f(x) = 0,$$

which means that $f(x) = -f(-x)$ holds for all reals x. In this case, we call f an *odd* function.

Example 5. Now, consider the functional equation

$$f(x + y) + f(x - y) = 2\max(f(x), f(y)),$$

where f is defined to be from $\mathbb{Q}$ to $\mathbb{Q}$. Let's call the given assertion $P(x, y)$. Take any two rationals x and y, and suppose, WLOG, that $f(x) \geq f(y)$. Then, $P(x, y)$ gives

$$f(x + y) + f(x - y) = 2f(x).$$

On the other hand, $P(y, x)$ yields

$$f(x + y) + f(y - x) = 2f(x).$$

Comparing, we see that $f(x - y) = f(y - x)$ for all $x, y \in \mathbb{Q}$. Now, let $a = x - y$ to obtain $f(a) = f(-a)$ for all $a \in \mathbb{Q}$. In this scenario, we say that f is an *even* function.

For easier referencing, I'm including the accurate definitions of even and odd functions here:

Definition 4 (Even Function). Suppose that A is a set with the property that if $a \in A$, then $-a \in A$. Let $f : A \to B$ be a function such that $f(x) = f(-x)$ for all $x \in A$. Then, we call f an *even* function.

Definition 5 (Odd Function). Suppose that A is a set with the property that if $a \in A$, then $-a \in A$. Let $f : A \to B$ be a function such that $f(x) = -f(-x)$ for all $x \in A$. Then, we call f an *odd* function.

If f is odd, then we can easily find by plugging $x = 0$ that $f(0) = 0$.

2.2.4 Involutive Functions

Definition 6. An *involutive* function, or simply an *involution*, is a function $f : A \to B$ such that $f(f(x)) = x$ happens for all $x \in A$. Notice that this directly implies $A = B$ and so f must be a surjection.

Example 6. If $f : A \to A$ is an involution, then f is a bijection because an involution is in fact a permutation, and hence f is a one-to-one and onto map. However, the converse is not necessarily true. Take for instance $f : \{0, 2, 4\} \to \{0, 2, 4\}$ defined by $f(n) = n + 2 \pmod 4$, for all $n \in A$. It is clear that $f(0) = 2$ and $f(f(0)) = f(2) = 4 \neq 0$.

Example 7. Suppose that $f : \mathbb{N} \to \mathbb{N}$ is an arithmetic function satisfying $f(x + f(y)) = f(x) + y$ for all positive integers x, y. Let's show that f is involutive. Let the given assertion be denoted by $P(x, y)$. Then, $P(x, y)$ and $P(y, x)$ give

$$f(x + f(y)) = y + f(x), \tag{2.2}$$
$$f(y + f(x)) = x + f(y). \tag{2.3}$$

Now, if you look closely:

$$x + f(y) \overset{f}{\mapsto} y + f(x) \overset{f}{\mapsto} x + f(y).$$

Now, if we can prove that every positive integer is representable as $x + f(y)$ for some $x \in \mathbb{Z}^{\geq 0}$ and $y \in \mathbb{N}$, then it implies that f is involutive. This is very easy for $n \geq 2$: to get $n = x + f(y)$, choose $y = 1$ and $x = n - f(1)$ (note that we want $x \geq 1$ to be in the domain of the function and that's why we should care about n being at least 2). So, we only need to prove that $f(1) = 1$. We now use an idea which is due to Gabriel (harazi). Let $P(x, y)$ be the assertion given in (2.2). Computing $P(x, 1)$ gives $f(x + f(1)) = 1 + f(x)$ and $P(f(1), x)$ gives $f(f(1) + f(x)) = x + f(f(1))$ for all $x \geq 1$. Now, $P(f(x), 1)$ implies

$$f(f(x) + f(1)) = 1 + f(f(x)).$$

Combining the latter two identities, we get

$$x + f(f(1)) = 1 + f(f(x)).$$

Hence, to show that $f(f(1)) = 1$, it suffices to find a natural x such that $f(f(x)) = x$. We have actually proved a much stronger thing: $f(f(x)) = x$ for all $x \geq 2$. So, $f(f(1)) = 1$ and we arrive to the conclusion that f is involutive, i.e., $f(f(x)) = x$ for all $x \geq 1$. Now, if we check $P(x, f(y))$, we see that f satisfies $f(x + y) = f(x) + f(y)$, i.e., f is an *additive* function. We discuss these functions as well as their solutions in the general case (when the domain is $\mathbb{Q}$ or $\mathbb{R}$) in section 2.3.

To sum it up, any additive involutive function f satisfies the functional equation in this example.

2.2.5   Functions Related to Integers

I didn't name this section *arithmetic functions* because, as we saw in section (2.2.2), an arithmetic function has the domain of only natural numbers. In this section, we study functions with a more general domain, say $\mathbb{R}$, that are somehow connected with integers. For instance,

Definition 7. The *floor* of x, denoted by $\lfloor x \rfloor$, is the largest integer smaller than or equal to x. So, if we let $f(x) = \lfloor x \rfloor$, then the domain of f is $\mathbb{R}$ and its image is $\mathbb{Z}$.

Example 8. The floor of 2.23 is 2, and the floor of -3.3 is -4.

Definition 8. The *fractional part* of a real number x is denoted by $\{x\}$, and defined as
$$\{x\} = x - \lfloor x \rfloor.$$
Hence, $\{x\}$ takes only values in the interval $[0,1)$. So, if we let $f(x) = \{x\}$, then f is a function from $\mathbb{R}$ to $[0,1)$.

Example 9. The fractional part of 3.98 is 0.98 and $\{n\} = 0$ for all integers n. Also, $\{-3.98\} = -3.98 - (-4) = 0.02$.

The functional equations in this set are not always nice and easy as $f(x) = x$ or $f(x) = x^3 + 3x$. As I said in the preface, there are problems in this book which are labeled as CIP – Crazy Invented Problems – exactly how Patrick (pco) abbreviates them. These problems were either really crazy invented problems randomly generated by enthusiast students, or were real problems in which the author made a mistake in writing the problem statement. For instance, someone would tell you "find all functions f..." instead of "find all continuous functions f." They simply miss one word "*continuous*" but that would totally ruin the problem, making it a CIP.

I wouldn't label the following example as a CIP, but it has the potential. The idea used in the example is by Patrick.

Example 10. Let's find all functions $f : \mathbb{R} \to \mathbb{R}$ that satisfy

$$P(x): \quad f(x) = f(\lfloor x \rfloor) + f(\{x\}) \tag{2.4}$$

for all reals x. As usual, we let this assertion to be $P(x)$. First, notice that we only need to know the values of $f(x)$ for $x \in \mathbb{Z}$ and $x \in (0,1)$ to know all the values of $f(x)$ for $x \in \mathbb{R}$. This is because for instance for $a_1 = 5.01$ and $a_2 = 5.02$, $P(x)$ would give

$$f(5.01) = f(5) + f(0.01),$$
$$f(5.02) = f(5) + f(0.02),$$

and so if we have the value of $f(n)$ for all $n \in \mathbb{Z}$ and also f of fractional parts $(x \in (0,1))$, then we can construct the whole domain $\mathbb{R}$. Now, $P(0)$ implies $f(0) = 0$. Let's make a claim:

Claim. The general solution to the functional equation in (2.4) is the following: let $g : \mathbb{Z} \to \mathbb{R}$ and $h : [0, 1) \to \mathbb{R}$ be arbitrary functions. Then,

$$f(x) = g(\lfloor x \rfloor) + h(\{x\}) - g(0) - h(0). \qquad (2.5)$$

Proof: One way is easy: let f be defined as in equation (2.5). To plug this into (2.4), we need $f(\lfloor x \rfloor)$ and $f(\{x\})$:

$$
\begin{aligned}
f(\lfloor x \rfloor) &= g(\lfloor \lfloor x \rfloor \rfloor) + h(\{\lfloor x \rfloor\}) - g(0) - h(0) \\
&= g(\lfloor x \rfloor) + h(0) - g(0) - h(0) \\
&= g(\lfloor x \rfloor) - g(0). \\
f(\{x\}) &= g(\lfloor \{x\} \rfloor) + h(\{\{x\}\}) - g(0) - h(0) \\
&= g(0) + h(\{\{x\}\}) - g(0) - h(0) \\
&= h(\{\{x\}\}) - h(0).
\end{aligned}
$$

Therefore,

$$
\begin{aligned}
f(x) &= f(\lfloor x \rfloor) + f(\{x\}) \\
&\iff g(\lfloor x \rfloor) + h(\{x\}) - g(0) - h(0) = g(\lfloor x \rfloor) - g(0) + h(\{\{x\}\}) - h(0) \\
&\iff 0 = 0,
\end{aligned}
$$

which is true. For the converse, remember that we only need $f(x)$ for $x \in \mathbb{Z} \cup (0, 1)$ to construct f over $\mathbb{R}$. Hence, we can write f as a combination of two functions, one giving the domain for integers, and the other one covers the interval $(0, 1)$. The essence of the idea is that since you can choose these two parts completely separately, therefore choosing

$$f(\lfloor x \rfloor) = g(\lfloor x \rfloor) - g(0) \text{ and } f(\{x\}) = h(\{\{x\}\}) - h(0),$$

where g and h can be any functions as in the claim. Adding these two, we get the desired form. The proof is complete.

2.2.6 The Bad Gu*i*, Complex Numbers, and Roots of Unity

The unit imaginary number i is defined as $i = \sqrt{-1}$, which is a bad thing according to elementary school students. We build a two-dimensional space using this bad guy and our good friend 1. That is, we define the space of *complex numbers* $\mathbb{C}$ as the set of all numbers of the form $a + ib$, where a and b are reals and i is the imaginary unit.

Definition 9. Let n be a positive integer. An *n*th *root of unity* is a complex number z such that $z^n = 1$ holds.

Example 11. i is a fourth root of unity. Same is true for $-i$, -1, and 1. Those are the only fourth roots of unity. In general, by Euler's amazing formula

$$e^{i\pi} = -1,$$

we can see that $e^{2\pi i k/n}$ is an nth root of unity (for $k = 0, 1, \ldots, n$).

2.3   Classical Functional Equations

2.3.1   Cauchy's Functional Equation

Definition 10 (Additive Function). A function $f : A \to B$ is called *additive* if

$$f(a_1 + a_2) = f(a_1) + f(a_2)$$

holds for all a_1 and a_2 such that $a_1, a_2, a_1 + a_2 \in A$

We consider the situation that $A = B = \mathbb{R}$. By using induction, it's easy to check

$$f(n) = nf(1),$$

for all $n \in \mathbb{Z}$ For rationals, we have

$$f\left(\frac{p}{q}\right) = \frac{1}{q}f(p) = \frac{p}{q}f(1).$$

The first equality follows from $f(nx) = nf(x)$, which can also be proved by induction. Now, we may expect that $f(x) = xf(1)$ for all $x \in \mathbb{R}$. However, it's false! (can you guess why?) Fortunately, we can add a few conditions to the functions to make the latter statement true.

Theorem 1 (Solutions for Cauchy's Functional Equation). An additive $f : \mathbb{R} \to \mathbb{R}$ is linear if any of the following conditions are met:

- f is continuous on some interval.

- f is bounded on some interval.

- f is monotonic on some interval.

Proof. For the first one, notice that if f is continuous at one point, then f is continuous everywhere. Next, for any real r, choose a sequence of rationals $\{a_n\}_{n\geq 1}$ converging to that number. Since f is continuous,

$$f(rx) = \lim_{n\to\infty} f(a_n x) = \lim_{n\to\infty} a_n f(x) = rf(x).$$

For the second one, suppose there is a real r such that $f(r) \neq rf(1)$. WLOG, assume that f is increasing and $f(r) > rf(1)$. Choose a rationals q so that $\frac{f(r)}{f(1)} > q > r$. Then,

$$f(r) < f(q) = qf(1) < f(r),$$

a contradiction.

For the third, let a_n be any rationals such that $nx - a_n \in [a, b]$. Then

$$
\begin{aligned}
|f(nx - a_n)| &= |n(f(x) - xf(1)) - (a_n - nx)f(1)| \\
&\geq n|f(x) - xf(1)| - |(nx - a_n)f(1)|,
\end{aligned}
$$

which means $f(x)$ must be equal to $xf(1)$. □

Once we have the solutions to additive Cauchy's functional equation, we can solve a wide variety of functional equations by defining new functions. For instance, let us try proving the following theorem:

Theorem 2. Let $f : \mathbb{R} \to \mathbb{R}^+$ be a monotone function which satisfies

$$f(x + y) = f(x)f(y)$$

for all reals x and y. Then, $f(x) = a^x$ for all $x \in \mathbb{R}$, where a can be any real number.

Proof. The key is to define $g : \mathbb{R} \to \mathbb{R}$ by $g(x) = \log f(x)$, where we suppose the logarithm to be in base e (or any other base that you want). Notice that this function is well-defined since f takes positive values. It is a good exercise for you to prove that the composition of two monotone functions is also monotone. Therefore, since both logarithm and f are monotone, then so is g. Since $g(x) = \log f(x)$, we find that $f(x) = e^{g(x)}$ and the given equation becomes

$$e^{g(x+y)} = e^{g(x)} \cdot e^{g(y)} = e^{g(x)+g(y)}.$$

Since the exponential function is injective, we then get

$$g(x + y) = g(x) + g(y).$$

This is now in a shape that we can apply Theorem (1) to. We obtain $g(x) = cx$ for all $x \in \mathbb{R}$, where c can be any real number. Plugging this back into $f(x) = e^{g(x)}$, we find that

$$f(x) = e^{cx} = a^x, \quad \forall x \in \mathbb{R},$$

where $a = e^c$. This finishes the proof. □

Equation	Transformation	Solution
$f(x+y) = f(x)f(y)$	$g(x) = \log f(x)$	a^x
$f(xy) = f(x)f(y)$	$g(x) = \log f(a^x)$	$x^{\log_a b}$
$f(xy) = f(x) + f(y)$	$g(x) = f(a^x)$	$\log_a x$
$f(x+y) = f(x) + f(y) + a$	$g(x) = f(x) + a$	$cx - a$
$f(x+y+a) = f(x) + f(y)$	$g(x) = f(x+a)$	$c(x+a)$
$f(x+y+a) = f(x) + f(y) + b$	$g(x) = f(x+a) + b$	$c(x+a) - b$

Table 2.1: Useful transformations.

The reader can easily check other functional equations and try to find suitable change of functions in order to reach the basic additive Cauchy's functional equation. That is actually how we solve a large amount of functional equations problems in mathematical contests!

I'm listing a couple of useful change of functions in Table (2.1) for your later reference. I got this table from the notes of Pang-Cheng Wu and Ting-Wei Chao on Functional Equations. Please try to work each case out and convince yourself that it works (you should consider appropriate conditions on the given equation).

2.3.2 Jensen's Functional Equation

Theorem 3 (Jensen's Functional Equation). Suppose that a function $f : \mathbb{R} \to \mathbb{R}$ is continuous and satisfies Jensen's functional equation:

$$\frac{f(x) + f(y)}{2} = f\left(\frac{x+y}{2}\right), \quad \forall x, y \in \mathbb{R}. \tag{2.6}$$

Then, f is linear. That is, we have $f(x) = ax + b$ for all $x \in \mathbb{R}$, where a and b can be any two reals.

Proof. As explained in previous parts, we must be looking for a method to transform this functional equation into Cauchy's additive form. First, notice that if $f(x)$ satisfies (2.6), then so does $g(x) = f(x) - b$ for any real c:

$$\frac{f(x) - b + f(y) - b}{2} = f\left(\frac{x+y}{2}\right) - b.$$

So, take $b = f(0)$, so that we have $g(0) = 0$ and g satisfies

$$\frac{g(x) + g(y)}{2} = g\left(\frac{x+y}{2}\right), \quad \forall x, y \in \mathbb{R}. \tag{2.7}$$

Let $P(x,y)$ be the assertion given in (2.7). Then, $P(x,0)$ implies $g(x) = 2g(x/2)$ for all reals x. Now, in the latter equation, use the change of variables $x \mapsto x+y$ to observe

$$g(x+y) = 2g\left(\frac{x+y}{2}\right), \quad \forall x, y \in \mathbb{R}. \tag{2.8}$$

Combining (2.7) and (2.8), we find that

$$g(x) + g(y) = g(x+y), \quad \forall x, y \in \mathbb{R}.$$

We arrived to Cauchy's additive function! So, $g(x) = ax$ for all $x \in \mathbb{R}$, where a is an arbitrary real number. Plugging this back into $f(x) = g(x) + b$, we find $f(x) = ax + b$, which is what we wanted to prove. □

2.3.3   General Solutions

In the world of functional equations, it is very important to fully comprehend the basic definitions. I am thankful to pco for providing the following examples to explain the meaning of the phrase "general solution."

Definition 11 (General Solution). A *general solution* to a functional equation is in fact a family of solutions to the equation which respects these two conditions:

- Any function in the given form indeed is a solution, and

- Any solution can be written in the given form.

With this definition, it is obvious that many apparently different (but in fact equivalent) general solutions may exist for a single functional equation.

Example 12. If we want to find all functions $f : \mathbb{R} \to \mathbb{R}$ such that

$$f(x) = f(-x), \quad \forall x \in \mathbb{R}. \tag{2.9}$$

Then a general solution is:

$f(x) = g(x)$ (for all $x \in \mathbb{R}$), where $g(x)$ is any even function.

The above sentence is a joke, but still a good one because it indeed satisfies the two given conditions in the definition (wise pco!). We can express this general solution in other forms as well. Here is one:

Let $g : \mathbb{R} \to \mathbb{R}$ be any function. Define $f(x)$ as

$$f(x) = \begin{cases} g(x), & \text{if } x \geq 0, \\ g(-x), & \text{if } x < 0. \end{cases}$$

Yet two other general solutions for (2.9):

$$f(x) = g(|x|), \text{ where } g : \mathbb{R} \to \mathbb{R} \text{ may be any function.}$$

and

$$f(x) = g(x) + g(-x), \text{ where } g : \mathbb{R} \to \mathbb{R} \text{ may be any function.}$$

You must be careful not to make a mistake when dealing with general solutions. You should choose a form for you general solution that respects **both** conditions. Here is a solution to (2.9) which looks like a general solution, but **in fact isn't a general solution**:

$$f(x) = g(x)g(-x), \text{ where } g : \mathbb{R} \to \mathbb{R} \text{ may be any function.} \qquad (2.10)$$

Why is this not a general solution? If you compute $f(-x)$ using the above equation, you will see that it is indeed equal to $f(x)$. **However**, we cannot write all solutions to (2.9) in the form (2.10). Take for example $f(x) = x^2 - 1$, which is an even function but there is no function g such that $f(x) = g(x)g(-x)$.

Note. You should now be able to explain why the following expression **doesn't make sense**:

... and hence the general solution to this equation is ...

There is no 'unique" general solution. Anything you find is just a general form. So, it is **better** to say

... so, the general solutions look like...

or

... therefore, a general solution to the equation is ...

2.3.4   Deviation from the Classical Equations

There are many possible variations of the classical functional equations. Throughout the problems in this book, you will see a very wide range of questions and a lot of cool ideas to crack the problems.

I would like to finish this chapter with a problem of APMO 2002. The idea in the solution is by Navneel Singhal.

Example 13. We are going to find out how to transform the functional equation

$$f(x^4 + y) = x^3 f(x) + f(f(y)), \qquad (2.11)$$

defined from $\mathbb{R}$ to $\mathbb{R}$, to the classical Cauchy's equation. Let's denote the assertion (2.11) by $P(x, y)$. Then, $P(0, x)$ yields $f(x) = f(f(x))$ for all $x \in \mathbb{R}$ and $P(x, 1)$ and $P(1, x^4)$ give

$$f(x^4 + 1) = x^3 f(x) + f(f(1)) = x^3 f(x) + f(1),$$
$$f(1 + x^4) = f(1) + f(f(x^4)) = f(1) + f(x^4).$$

Hence, $x^3 f(x) = f(x^4)$ holds for all $x \in \mathbb{R}$. Now, using $P(\sqrt[4]{x}, y)$ for $x \geq 0$, we find that $f(x + y) = f(x) + f(y)$, which is the Cauchy's additive formula. We now need to somehow remove the $x \geq 0$ condition. Since there is no condition on y, choose $y = -x$. Then, $f(0) = f(x) + f(-x)$ and hence f is odd. Therefore, for the choice of $x = -a < 0$ we have

$$
\begin{aligned}
f(x + y) &= f(-a + y) \\
&= -f(a - y) \\
&= -(f(a) + f(-y)) && \text{(since } a > 0\text{)} \\
&= -(-f(-a) - f(y)) && \text{(since } f \text{ is odd)} \\
&= -(-f(x) - f(y)) && \text{(since } x = -a\text{)} \\
&= f(x) + f(y).
\end{aligned}
$$

This means that f satisfies the classical additive Cauchy equation for $x, y \in \mathbb{R}$.

Chapter 3

Problems

3.1   Functions Over $\mathbb{C}$

Problem 1.

Let

$$f(x) = \begin{cases} z, & \text{if } \Re(z) \geq 0, \\ -z, & \text{if } \Re(z) < 0, \end{cases}$$

be a function defined on $\mathbb{C}$. A sequence $\{z_n\}$ is defined as $z_1 = u$ and for all $n \geq 1$,

$$z_{n+1} = f\left(z_n^2 + z_n + 1\right).$$

Given $\{z_n\}$ is periodic, find all possible values of u.

Problem 2.

Consider the functional equation $af(z) + bf(w^2 z) = g(z)$, where w is a complex cube root of unity, a and b are fixed complex numbers, and $g(z)$ is a known complex function. Prove that the complex function $f(z)$ can be uniquely determined if $a^3 + b^3 \neq 0$.

3.2   Functions Over $\mathbb{R}$

3.2.1   Cauchy-type and Jensen-type

Problem 3.
Find all functions $f : \mathbb{R} \to \mathbb{R}$ satisfying

$$fx^2 + yf(z)) = xf(x) + zf(y)$$

for all reals x, y, z.

Problem 4.
Find all functions $f : \mathbb{R} \to \mathbb{R}$ such that for any $x, y \in \mathbb{R}$,

$$f(x) + f(x + f(y)) = y + f(f(x) + f(f(y))).$$

Problem 5.
Find all continuous functions $f : \mathbb{R} \to \mathbb{R}$ such that

$$\frac{f(x+y)}{f(x-y)} = \frac{f(x) + f(y)}{f(x) - f(y)},$$

for all reals x and y such that $x \neq y$.

Problem 6.
Find all functions $f : \mathbb{R} \to \mathbb{R}$ such that for some $a, b \in \mathbb{R}$,

$$f(x)f(y) = x^a f\left(\frac{y}{2}\right) + y^b f\left(\frac{x}{2}\right)$$

holds for all reals x and y.

Problem 7 (*IMO 1983*).
Find all functions $f : \mathbb{R}^+ \to \mathbb{R}^+$ satisfying $f(xf(y)) = yf(x)$ for all positive reals x and y, and $\lim_{x\to\infty} f(x) = 0$.

3.2.2   Continuity

Problem 8 (*Romanian National Olympiad 2018, Grade 11, Problem 3 – Proposed by Julieta R. Vergulescu*).
Let $f : \mathbb{R} \to \mathbb{R}$ be a function with the intermediate value property. If f is injective on $\mathbb{R} \setminus \mathbb{Q}$, prove that f is continuous on $\mathbb{R}$.

Problem 9.
Find all continuous functions $f : \mathbb{R} \to \mathbb{R}$ such that

$$f(x+y)f(x-y) = (f(x)f(y))^2, \quad \forall x, y \in \mathbb{R}.$$

Problem 10.
Find all continuous functions $f : \mathbb{R} \to \mathbb{R}$ such that

$$f(f(x + y)) = f(x) + f(y)$$

for all reals x and y.

Problem 11.
Find all continuous functions $f : \mathbb{R} \to \mathbb{R}$ such that:

$$f(x - f(y)) = f(x) - y$$

for all real numbers x, y.

Problem 12.
Find all continuous functions $f : \mathbb{R} \to \mathbb{R}$ such that

$$f(x) = f(x + 1) = f(x + \sqrt{2})$$

for all $x \in \mathbb{R}$.

Problem 13.
Find all continuous functions $f : \mathbb{R} \to \mathbb{R}$ such that

$$f(xy) + f(x + y) = f(xy + x) + f(y)$$

for all real numbers x, y.

Problem 14.
A function $f : \mathbb{R} \to \mathbb{R}$ is said to have the property P if it is continuous and

$$2f(f(x) = 3f(x) - x, \quad \forall x \in \mathbb{R}.$$

1. Prove that
$$M = \{x \in \mathbb{R} : f(x) = x\}$$
   is an non-empty interval.

2. Find all functions with the property P.

Problem 15 (*Vojtěch Jarník International Mathematical Competition 2017, Category I, Problem 1*).
Let $f : \mathbb{R} \to \mathbb{R}$ be a continuous function satisfying

$$f(x + 2y) = 2f(x)f(y)$$

for every $x, y \in \mathbb{R}$. Prove that f is constant.

Problem 16 (*2017 Moldova TST, Day 2, Problem 1*).
Find all continuous functions $f : \mathbb{R} \to \mathbb{R}$ such, that

$$f(xy) = f\left(\frac{x^2 + y^2}{2}\right) + (x - y)^2$$

for any real numbers x and y.

3.2.3   Injective, Surjective, and Monotone Functions

Problem 17.
A function $f : \mathbb{R} \to \mathbb{R}$ is called *Patrician* if it satisfies

$$f(yf(x + y) + x) = f(y)^2 + f((x - 1)f(y))$$

for all $x, y \in \mathbb{R}$.

1. Find all injective Patrician functions.

2. Find all surjective Patrician functions.

3. Show that there exist an infinite family of Patrician functions which
   are non-constant, non-injective, and non-surjective.

4. *[CIP alert]* Find all Patrician functions.

Problem 18 (*Uzbekistan Math Olympiad 2018, Problem 3*).
Find all monotone functions $f : \mathbb{R} \to \mathbb{R}$ such that $f(2018x) = f(x) + 2017x$
for all real numbers x.

Problem 19 (*Romanian National Olympiad 2018, Grade 10, Problem 1*).
Let $n \in \mathbb{N}_{\geq 2}$ and $a_1, a_2, \ldots, a_n \in (1, \infty)$. Prove that $f : [0, \infty) \to \mathbb{R}$ with

$$f(x) = (a_1 a_2 \ldots a_n)^x - a_1^x - a_2^x - \ldots - a_n^x$$

is a strictly increasing function.

Problem 20.
Let $f : \mathbb{R} \to \mathbb{R}$ be a function such that

$$f(a + 2f(a)f(b)) = f(a) + 2af(b)$$

for all reals a and b. Also, suppose that f is not the all-zero function.

1. Prove that f is surjective.

2. Find all such f.

Problem 21 (*Proposed by Mohammad Jafari*).
In each of the following parts, if $f : \mathbb{R}^+ \to \mathbb{R}^+$ is a function that satisfies the given condition for all positive reals x and y, show that f is injecive.

1. $f(f(x) + f(y)) = f(2x) - f(x) + f(2y) - y$.

2. $f(f(3x) + 3f(y)) = x + 2f(x) + f(3y)$.

3. $f(3xy) = 2f(xy) + xf(y)$.

4. $f(3x + f(y)) = f(2x) + x + 2f(y) - y$.

5. $f(x + 2f(x) + f(3y)) = 3f(x) + y + 2f(y)$.

Problem 22 (*Turkey Team Selection Test 2018, Problem 2*).
Find all surjective functions $f : \mathbb{R} \to \mathbb{R}$ such that

$$f(xf(y) + y^2) = f((x + y)^2) - xf(x)$$

for all real numbers x, y.

Problem 23.
Find all functions $f : \mathbb{R} \to \mathbb{R}$ such that

$$(x - 2) \cdot f(y) + f(y + 2 \cdot f(x)) = f(x + y \cdot f(x))$$

holds for all reals x and y.

Problem 24 (*Proposed by Mohammad Jafari*).
Find all functions $f, g : \mathbb{R}^+ \to \mathbb{R}^+$ that satisfy

$$f(g(x) + g(2y)) = g(x) + 3f(y) - y, \text{ and}$$
$$g(2f(x) + 2g(y)) = 3f(x) - x + g(2y),$$

for all positive reals x and y and $g(x)$ is injective.

Problem 25 (*Vietnam National Olympiad 2017*).
Find all functions $f : \mathbb{R} \to \mathbb{R}$ satisfying the relation

$$f(xf(y) - f(x)) = 2f(x) + xy$$

for all $x, y \in \mathbb{R}$.

Problem 26.
Given real number $a \notin \{-1, 0, 1\}$, find all functions $f : \mathbb{R} \to \mathbb{R}$ such that

$$f(f(x) + ay) = (a^2 + a)x + f(f(y) - x)$$

for all reals x and y.

Problem 27.
Find all functions $f : \mathbb{R} \to \mathbb{R}$ such that

$$f(f(x) - xf(y)) + xy = 2f(x)$$

for all $x, y \in \mathbb{R}$.

Problem 28 (*Greece TST 2017, Problem 3*).
Find all functions $f, g : \mathbb{R} \to \mathbb{R}$ such that

$$f(x - 3f(y)) = xf(y) - yf(x) + g(x), \quad \forall x, y \in \mathbb{R},$$

and $g(1) = -8$.

Problem 29 (*Lotus Olympiad 2017 – Proposed by Murad Aghazade*).
Find all functions $f : \mathbb{R}^+ \to \mathbb{R}^+$ such that

$$(x^2 + y^2)f(2017xf(y) + f(f(y))f(x)) = x^3 f(f(f(x))f(y))$$

for all $x, y \in \mathbb{R}^+$.

Problem 30.
Determine all functions $f : \mathbb{R}^+ \to \mathbb{R}^+$ such that

$$f(x + f(x)f(y)) = f(x) + xf(y), \quad \forall x, y \in \mathbb{R}^+.$$

3.2.4   Existence

Problem 31.
Prove that there exists no function $f : \mathbb{R} \to \mathbb{R}$ satisfying

$$f(x + y) = e^x f(y) + e^y f(x) + xy, \quad \forall x, y \in \mathbb{R}.$$

Problem 32.
Prove that there exist infinitely many functions f defined on $\mathbb{N}$ such that for all $n, k \in \mathbb{N}$, the following equation holds:

$$f(nf(k) + kf(n)) = f(n^2 + k^2)f(n + k - 1).$$

Problem 33.
Does there exist a function f (defined on reals) which is continuous at the point $x = 0$ and $nf(nx) = f(x) + nx$, for a given integer $n \geq 2$ and all reals x?

Problem 34 (*Vojtěch Jarník International Mathematical Competition 2017, Category II, Problem 2*).
Prove or disprove the following statement: if $g : (0,1) \to (0,1)$ is an increasing function and satisfies $g(x) > x$ for all $x \in (0,1)$, then there exists a continuous function $f : (0,1) \to \mathbb{R}$ satisfying $f(x) < f(g(x))$ for all $x \in (0,1)$, but f is not an increasing function.

Problem 35.
Prove that there is no function $f : \mathbb{R}^+ \to \mathbb{R}$ such that the inequality

$$f(x+y) > y(f(x)^2)$$

holds for all positive x, y,

3.2.5 Trigonometric and Periodic Functions

Problem 36 (*IMO Shortlist 1996, A7*).
Let $f : \mathbb{R} \to \mathbb{R}$ be a function such that $|f(x)| \leq 1$ for all $x \in \mathbb{R}$ and

$$f\left(x + \frac{13}{42}\right) + f(x) = f\left(x + \frac{1}{6}\right) + f\left(x + \frac{1}{7}\right).$$

Prove that f is a periodic function (that is, there exists a non-zero real number c such $f(x+c) = f(x)$ for all $x \in \mathbb{R}$).

Problem 37.
Find all functions $f : \mathbb{R} \to \mathbb{R}$ such that $f(3x+2) + f(3x+29) = 0$ for any real x.

Problem 38 (*CIP alert*).
Does there exist a surjective and periodic function f on reals so that

$$f(x+1) - f(x) = c$$

holds for all $x \in \mathbb{R}$, where c is a fixed real number?

Problem 39.
Given real number $a \notin \{-1, 0, 1\}$, find all functions $f : \mathbb{R} \to \mathbb{R}$ such that

$$f(f(x) + ay) = (a^2 + a)x + f(f(y) - x)$$

for all reals x and y.

3.2.6 Functions Combined with Polynomials

Problem 40 (*Hong Kong Pre-IMO Mock Exam 2017*).
Let d be a non-negative integer. Determine all functions $f : \mathbb{R}^2 \to \mathbb{R}$ such that, for any real constants A, B, C, and D, $f(At+B, Ct+D)$ is a polynomial in t of degree at most d.

Problem 41 (*Proposed by Mohammad Jafari*).
Let $g(x)$ be a polynomial with real coefficients. Find all functions $f : \mathbb{R} \to \mathbb{R}$ that satisfy
$$\lfloor f(xg(x^2)) \rfloor = \lfloor f(g(x))^2 \rfloor + 1397$$
for all $x \in \mathbb{R}$.

Problem 42.
Let $p(x)$ be a polynomial with integer coefficients. Define a sequence $\{a_n\}$ such that $a_0 = 0$ and $a_{n+1} = p(a_n)$ for all $n \in \mathbb{N}$. Suppose that there is a positive integer m with $a_m = 0$. Prove that $a_1 = 0$ or $a_2 = 0$.

Problem 43.
Find all functions $f : \mathbb{R} \to \mathbb{R}$ which satisfy

  (i) $f(x + y) = f(x) + f(y)$ for all real x, y, and

  (ii) $f(p(x)) = p(f(x))$ for some polynomial $p(x)$ of degree ≥ 2.

Problem 44 (*Iran TST 2017, Second Exam, Day 2, Problem 4 – Proposed by Alireza Shavali*).
A $n + 1$-tuple $(h_1, h_2, \ldots, h_{n+1})$, where $h_i(x_1, x_2, \ldots, x_n)$ is a n variable polynomials with real coefficients (for $i = 1, 2, \ldots, n + 1$) is called *good* if the following condition holds: for any n functions $f_1, f_2, \ldots, f_n : \mathbb{R} \to \mathbb{R}$, if for all $1 \leq i \leq n + 1$,

$$P_i(x) = h_i(f_1(x), f_2(x), \ldots, f_n(x))$$

is a polynomial in the variable x, then $f_1(x), f_2(x), \ldots, f_n(x)$ are polynomials.

a) Prove that for all positive integers n, there exists a good $n + 1$-tuple $(h_1, h_2, \ldots, h_{n+1})$ such that the degree of h_i is more than 1 for all i.

b) Prove that there doesn't exist any integer $n > 1$ that for which there is a good $n + 1$-tuple $(h_1, h_2, \ldots, h_{n+1})$ such that all h_i are symmetric polynomials.

3.2.7 Functions on $\mathbb{R}^+$

Problem 45 (*Proposed by Mohammad Jafari*).
For all functions $f, g : \mathbb{R}^+ \to \mathbb{R}^+$ that satisfy $f(1) = g(1)$ and for all positive x and y,

$$f(g(x) + y) = f(x) + g(y), \text{ and}$$
$$g(f(x) + y) = g(x) + f(y).$$

Prove that $f(x) = g(x)$ for all $x \in \mathbb{R}^+$.

Problem 46 (*Proposed by Mohammad Jafari*).
Find all functions $f, g : \mathbb{R}^+ \to \mathbb{R}^+$ that satisfy

$$f(x + g(x) + y) = g(x) + f(x) + f(y), \text{ and}$$
$$g(x + f(x) + y) = f(x) + g(x) + g(y),$$

for all positive reals x and y.

Problem 47 (*Proposed by Mohammad Jafari*).
Find all functions $f : \mathbb{R}^+ \to \mathbb{R}^+$ for which the equation

$$f(f(x) + 2y) = f(2x + y) + 2y$$

holds for all positive reals x and y.

Problem 48 (*Proposed by Mohammad Jafari*).
Find all functions $f : \mathbb{R}^+ \to \mathbb{R}^+$ that satisfy

$$f(x + 2f(x) + 3y) = f(3x) + y + 2f(y)$$

for all $x, y \in \mathbb{R}^+$.

Problem 49 (*Proposed by Mohammad Jafari – Posted on March 20, 2018*).
Find all functions $f, g : \mathbb{R}^+ \to \mathbb{R}^+$ that satisfy

$$f(x + y) = g(x)g(y)^2 + g(y)g(x)^2, \text{ and}$$
$$g(x + y) = f(x)f(y)^2 + f(y)f(x)^2,$$

for all positive reals x and y.

Problem 50 (*Kazakhstan Math Olympiad 2018, Grade 10, P3*).
Find all functions $f : \mathbb{R}^+ \to \mathbb{R}^+$ such that for all $x, y \in \mathbb{R}^+$,

$$f(3f(xy)^2 + (xy)^2) = (xf(y) + yf(x))^2.$$

Problem 51.
Find all functions $f : \mathbb{R}^+ \to \mathbb{R}^+$ such that

$$f(x + f(y)) = f(x) - x + f(x + y)$$

for all positive real numbers x, y.

Problem 52.
Find all functions $f : \mathbb{R}^+ \to \mathbb{R}^+$ satisfying

$$f\left(f(xy) - xy\right) + xf(y) + yf(x) = f(xy) + f(x)f(y), \quad \forall x, y \in \mathbb{R}^+.$$

Problem 53.
Prove that there are no functions $f : \mathbb{R}^+ \to \mathbb{R}^+$ such that

$$(x + y)f(f(x)y) = x^2 f(f(x) + f(y)), \quad \forall x, y \in \mathbb{R}^+.$$

Problem 54.
Find all functions $f : \mathbb{R}^+ \to \mathbb{R}$ that satisfy

$$f(x - y)^2 = f(x)^2 - 2f(xy) + f(y)^2$$

for all real x and y with $x > y > 0$.

Problem 55 (*Similar to Problem 90*).
Find all functions $f, g : \mathbb{R}^+ \to \mathbb{R}^+$ such that

$$f(x + f(y)) = \{y\} + g(x)$$

holds for all positive reals x and y.

Problem 56 (*Albania BMO TST 2017, Problem 3*).
Find all functions $f : \mathbb{R}^+ \to \mathbb{R}^+$ such that

$$f(x)f(y)f(z) = 9f(z + xyf(z)),$$

where x, y, and z, can be any three positive real numbers.

Problem 57 (*Belarus Mathematical Olympiad 2017*).
Find all functions $f : \mathbb{R}^+ \to \mathbb{R}^+$ satisfying the equation

$$f(x + f(xy)) = xf(1 + f(y))$$

for all positive x and y.

Problem 58 (*IMO Shortlist 2016, Estonia IMO TST Contest 1 – Proposed by Estonia*).
Find all functions $f : \mathbb{R}^+ \to \mathbb{R}^+$ such that for any $x, y \in \mathbb{R}^+$, we have

$$xf(x^2)f(f(y)) + f(yf(x)) = f(xy)\left(f(f(x^2)) + f(f(y^2)))\right).$$

Problem 59 (*Saudi Arabia Mock Tests for BMO 2017, Problem 2*).
Find all functions $f : \mathbb{R}^+ \to \mathbb{R}$ such that for all positive real numbers x and y, the following conditions are satisfied:

(i) $2f(x) + 2f(y) \le f(x + y)$, and

(ii) $(x + y)(yf(x) + xf(y)) \ge xyf(x + y)$.

Problem 60.
Find all functions $f : \mathbb{R}^+ \to \mathbb{R}$ such that

$$f(x + y)^2 = f(x)^2 + 2f(xy) + f(y)^2,$$

for all $x, y \in \mathbb{R}^+$.

Problem 61.
Find all functions $f : \mathbb{R}^+ \to \mathbb{R}^+$ such that for all $x, y \in \mathbb{R}^+$ we have

$$f(f(x) + x + y) = x\left(1 + xf\left(\frac{1}{x + y}\right)\right).$$

Problem 62.
Find all functions $f : \mathbb{R}^+ \to \mathbb{R}^+$ such that:

$$f\left(\frac{x + y}{2}\right) = \frac{2f(x)f(y)}{f(x) + f(y)}$$

holds for all positive reals x and y.

3.2.8   Sequences

Problem 63 (*CIP alert*).
Find an infinite family of functions $f : \mathbb{R} \to \mathbb{R}$ which are solutions to

$$(f(1 + 2x))^2 = x - (f(1 - x))^3$$

for all real x.

Problem 64 (*Proposed by Mohammad Jafari*).
Find all functions $f : \mathbb{R}^+ \to \mathbb{R}^+$ that satisfy

$$f(x + f(x) + y) = x + f(x) + 3y - 2f(y), \quad \forall x, y \in \mathbb{R}^+.$$

Problem 65.
Find all functions f defined om $\mathbb{R}^+$ such that $f(0) = 0$ and

$$f(x) = 1 + 7f\left(\left\lfloor \frac{x}{2} \right\rfloor\right) - 6f\left(\left\lfloor \frac{x}{4} \right\rfloor\right)$$

for all $x > 0$.

Problem 66.
Find all functions $f : \mathbb{R}^+ \to \mathbb{R}^+$ such that

$$f(2016 + xf(y)) = yf(x + y + 2016),$$

for all $x, y \in \mathbb{R}^+$.

3.2.9 Inequalities

Problem 67 (*Bulgaria 2015, Problem 4*).
Find all functions $f : \mathbb{R}^+ \to \mathbb{R}^+$ such that for all $x, y \in R^+$, the following conditions are satisfied:

(i) $f(x + y) \geq f(x) + y$, and

(ii) $f(f(x)) \leq x$.

Problem 68.
Find all functions $f : \mathbb{R}^+ \to \mathbb{R}$ satisfying the inequality

$$f(x) - f(y) \geq \ln\left(\frac{x}{y}\right) + x - y$$

for all $x, y \in \mathbb{R}^+$.

Problem 69.
Find all real numbers a and functions $f : \mathbb{R} \to \mathbb{R}$ which satisfy the following conditions:

(i) $af(x) - x \leq af(f(y)) - y$ holds for all real numbers x and y.

(ii) there is a real number x_0 is such that $f(x_0) = x_0$.

Problem 70.
Find all functions $f : \mathbb{R}^+ \to \mathbb{R}$ satisfying

$$f(x) + f(y) \leq \frac{f(x+y)}{4}, \text{ and}$$
$$\frac{f(x)}{y} + \frac{f(y)}{x} \geq \left(\frac{1}{x} + \frac{1}{y}\right) \cdot \frac{f(x+y)}{8},$$

for all positive reals x, y.

Problem 71.
Does there exist a function $f : [0, 2017] \to \mathbb{R}$ such that

$$f(x + y^2) \geq y + f(x)$$

for all x, y with $x \in [0, 2017]$ and $x + y^2 \in [0, 2017]$?

Problem 72 (*Kosovo Mathematical Olympiad 2018 – Proposed by Dorlir Ahmeti*).
Find all functions $f : \mathbb{R} \to \mathbb{R}$ such that

$$f(x + y) + yf(x) \leq x + f(y) + f(xy)$$

holds for all real x, y.

Problem 73 (*Korean Mathematical Olympiad 2017, Problem 7*).
Find all real numbers c such that there exists a function $f : \mathbb{R}^+ \cup \{0\} \to \mathbb{R}$ which satisfies the following: for all non-negative reals x, y,

$$f(x + y^2) \geq cf(x) + y.$$

Problem 74 (*ELMO 2017, Problem 6 – Proposed by Ashwin Sah*).
Find all functions $f : \mathbb{R} \to \mathbb{R}$ such that for all real numbers $a, b,$ and c:

  (i) If $a + b + c \geq 0$ then $f(a^3) + f(b^3) + f(c^3) \geq 3f(abc)$.

  (ii) If $a + b + c \leq 0$ then $f(a^3) + f(b^3) + f(c^3) \leq 3f(abc)$.

3.2.10   Miscellaneous

Innovative Problems

Problem 75 (*KTOM April 2018*).
Find all function $f : \mathbb{R} \to \mathbb{R}$ so that

$$f(zf(x)f(y)) + f(f(z)(f(x) + f(y))) = f(xyz + xz + yz), \quad \forall x, y, z \in \mathbb{R}.$$

Problem 76.
A function f is non-decreasing in $[0, 1]$ and for every $x \in [0, 1]$, we have

$$f(x) + f(1 - x) = 1 \text{ and } f(x) = 2f\left(\frac{x}{3}\right).$$

Find $f\left(\frac{5}{8}\right)$.

Problem 77.
Find all functions f defined on $[-0.5, 0.5]$ such that

$$f\left(\frac{x}{x-1}\right) = \frac{f(x) - x}{1 - x}$$

for all $x \in [-0.5, 0.5]$.

Problem 78 (Macedonian Mathematical Olympiad 2018, Problem 3).
Determine all functions $f : \mathbb{R} \to \mathbb{R}$ such that:

$$f(\max\{x, y\} + \min\{f(x), f(y)\}) = x + y$$

for all real $x, y \in \mathbb{R}$

Problem 79.
Find all real numbers c for which there exists a function $f : \mathbb{R} \to \mathbb{R}$ such that for all $x, y \in \mathbb{R}$,

$$f(f(x) + f(y)) + cxy = f(x + y).$$

Problem 80 (*Iran TST 2018, Second Exam, Day 1, Problem 1 – Proposed by Navid Safaei*).
Find all functions $f : \mathbb{R} \to \mathbb{R}$ that satisfy the following conditions:

a. $x + f(y + f(x)) = y + f(x + f(y)), \quad \forall x, y \in \mathbb{R}.$

b. The set
$$I = \left\{ \frac{f(x) - f(y)}{x - y} \mid x, y \in \mathbb{R}, x \neq y \right\}$$
is an interval. That is, for any $a, b \in I$ such that $a < b$, we have $[a, b] \subseteq I$.

Problem 81 (*Romanian National Olympiad 2018, Grade 9, Problem 3*).
Let $f, g : \mathbb{R} \to \mathbb{R}$ be two quadratics such that for any real number r, if $f(r)$ is an integer, then $g(r)$ is also an integer. Prove that there are two integers m and n such that

$$g(x) = mf(x) + n, \quad \forall x \in \mathbb{R}.$$

Problem 82.
Find all functions $f : \mathbb{R} \to \mathbb{R}$ such that

$$f(x - f(y)) = f(x + y) + f(f(y) + y)$$

for all real numbers x, y.

Problem 83.
Find all functions $f : \mathbb{R} \to \mathbb{R}$ satisfying

$$f(x + f(y)) = f(y^2 + 3) + 2xf(y) + f(x) - 3$$

, for all $x, y \in \mathbb{R}$.

Problem 84.
Find all functions $f : \mathbb{R} \to \mathbb{R}$ that satisfy

$$f(x - f(y)) = f(x + y^{2016}) + 2016$$

for all reals x, y.

Problem 85 (*CIP alert*).
Determine all functions $f : \mathbb{R} \to \mathbb{R}$ such that, for all real numbers x and y,

$$f(f(x)f(y)) = f(x + y) + f(xy).$$

Problem 86 (*Austria 2017, Final Round, Part 2, Day 1, Problem 1 – Proposed by Walther Janous*).
Let α be a fixed real number. Find all functions $f : \mathbb{R} \to \mathbb{R}$ such that

$$f(f(x + y)f(x - y)) = x^2 + \alpha y f(y)$$

for all $x, y \in \mathbb{R}$.

Problem 87.
Find all functions $f : \mathbb{R} \to \mathbb{R}$ satisfying the following condition

$$(f(x))^2 + 2f(y - x)f(-y) = (f(-x))^2 + 2f(x - y)f(y),$$

for all $x, y \in \mathbb{R}$.

Problem 88.
For each real number t let $g(t)$ be the total number of functions $f : \mathbb{R} \to \mathbb{R}$ satisfying

$$f(xy + f(y)) = f(x)y + t$$

for all real numbers x, y. Determine the function $g(t)$.

Problem 89 (*Iran TST 2017, Third Exam, Day 1, Problem 3 – Proposed by Mojtaba Zare and Ali Daei Nabi*).
Find all functions $f : \mathbb{R}^+ \times \mathbb{R}^+ \to \mathbb{R}^+$ that satisfy

$$f\left(f(x,y),z\right) = x^2 y^2 f(x,z)$$

and

$$f\left(x, 1 + f(x,y)\right) \geq x^2 + xy f(x,x)$$

for all positive real numbers x, y, z.

Problem 90 (*Ukraine National Mathematical Olympiad 2017, Fourth Round, Day 2, Grade 11 – Proposed by Igor Voronovych – Similar to Problem 55*).
Do there exist functions $f, g : \mathbb{R} \to \mathbb{R}$ such that

$$f(x + f(y)) = \{y\} + g(x)$$

holds for all real x and y?

Problem 91 (*National Internet Math Olympiad 2017, Day 31, Problem 7 – Proposed by Ayush Kamat*).
Let the function $f(x) = \lfloor x \rfloor \{x\}$. Compute the smallest positive integer n such that the graph of $f(f(f(x)))$ on the interval $[0, n]$ is the union of 2017 or more line segments.

Problem 92 (*Turkey Team Selection Test 2017, Problem 7 (modified version)*).
Let a be a fixed real number. Find all functions $f : \mathbb{R} \to \mathbb{R}$ such that

$$f(xy + f(y)) = f(x)y + a$$

holds for every $x, y \in \mathbb{R}$.

Problem 93 (*Iran Summer Courses 2017*).
Is there a function $f : \mathbb{R} \to \mathbb{R}$ such that $f(f(x)) = x^2 + x + 3$ holds for all real x?

Problem 94.
Find all functions $f : \mathbb{R} \to \mathbb{R}$ such that for all reals x,

$$f(x + 2) - 2f(x + 1) + f(x) = x^2.$$

Problem 95.
Find all functions $f : \mathbb{R} \to \mathbb{R}$ such that

$$(x + y^2)f(yf(x)) = xyf(y^2 + f(x)),$$

for all $x, y \in \mathbb{R}$.

Problem 96.
Determine all functions $f : \mathbb{R} \to \mathbb{R}$ that satisfy

$$f(x^2 + f(y)) = f(f(x)) + 2f(xy) + f(y^2)$$

for all $x, y \in \mathbb{R}$.

Problem 97 (*All-Russian olympiad 1995, Grade 11, First Day, Problem 2 – Proposed by D. Tereshin*).
Prove that every real function, defined on all of $\mathbb{R}$, can be represented as a sum of two functions whose graphs both have an axis of symmetry.

Substitutions

Problem 98 (*Ukraine National Mathematical Olympiad 2017, Third Round, Day 2, Grade 10 – Proposed by Andriy Anikushin*).
Find all functions $f : \mathbb{R} \to \mathbb{R}$ such that

$$f(x + f(f(y))) = y + f(f(x))$$

for all real numbers x and y.

Problem 99 (*Australia 2017*).
Find all functions $f : \mathbb{R} \to \mathbb{R}$ such that

$$f(x^2 + f(y)) = f(xy)$$

for all reals x and y.

Problem 100 (*Uzbekistan TST 2018*).
Find all functions $f : \mathbb{R} \to \mathbb{R}$ such that

$$(a - b)f(a + b) + (b - c)f(b + c) + (c - a)f(c + a) = 0$$

for all $a, b, c \in \mathbb{R}$.

Problem 101.
Find al functions $f : \mathbb{R} \to \mathbb{R}$ such that for all reals x and y, we have $f(x + y) = f(x) + f(y)$ and $f(x^3) = x^2 f(x)$.

Problem 102.
Find all functions $f : \mathbb{R}^+ \to \mathbb{R}^+$ such that

$$f(x)f(y) = 2f(x + yf(x))$$

holds for all $x, y \in \mathbb{R}^+$.

Problem 103.
Find all functions $f : \mathbb{R} \to \mathbb{R}$ such that

$$f(x)f(xf(y)) = x^2 f(y)$$

holds for all real numbers x and y.

Problem 104.
Find all functions $f : \mathbb{R} \to \mathbb{R}$ such that for all $x, y \in \mathbb{R}$, we have

$$f(f(x+y)) = f(x+y) + f(x)f(y) - xy.$$

Problem 105.
Find all functions $f : \mathbb{R} \to \mathbb{R}$ such that

$$f(xf(y)) = (1-y)f(xy) + x^2 y^2 f(y)$$

holds for all reals x and y.

Problem 106.
Find all functions $f : \mathbb{R} \to \mathbb{R}$ such that

$$f(x+y) = f(x) + f(y) + f(xy)$$

for all $x, y \in \mathbb{R}$.

Problem 107.
Find all functions $f : \mathbb{R} \to \mathbb{R}$ such that

$$f(x^3) - f(y^3) = (x^2 + xy + y^2)(f(x) - f(y)).$$

Problem 108.
Find all functions $f : \mathbb{R} \to \mathbb{R}$ satisfying

$$f\left(f\left(x + f\left(y\right)\right) - y - f\left(x\right)\right) = xf\left(y\right) - yf\left(x\right)$$

for all real numbers x, y.

Problem 109.
Find all functions $f : \mathbb{R} \to \mathbb{R}$ such that

$$f\left(f\left(x+y\right) - x\right) f\left(f\left(x+y\right) - y\right) = xy$$

holds for all $x, y \in \mathbb{R}$.

Problem 110.
Find all functions $f : \mathbb{R} \to \mathbb{R}$ such that

$$(y + 1)f(x) + f(xf(y) + f(x + y)) = y$$

for all $x, y \in \mathbb{R}$.

Problem 111.
Find all functions $f : \mathbb{R} \to \mathbb{R}$ for which

$$f(x - f(y)) = f(x) - \lfloor y \rfloor$$

for all reals x, y.

Problem 112 (*Proposed by Mohammad Jafari*).
Find all functions $f : \mathbb{R} \to \mathbb{R}$ that satisfy for all real x the equation

$$\lfloor f(x^4 - 5x^2 + 2015)^3 \rfloor + \lfloor f(x^4 - 5x^2 + 2015) \rfloor = \lfloor x^4 + x^2 + 1 \rfloor.$$

Problem 113 (*2018 Korea Winter Program Practice Test 1, Problem 1*).
Find all functions $f : \mathbb{R} \to \mathbb{R}$ satisfying the following conditions:

1. $f(x + y) - f(x) - f(y) \in \{0, 1\}$ for all $x, y \in \mathbb{R}$, and

2. $\lfloor f(x) \rfloor = \lfloor x \rfloor$ for all real x.

Problem 114.
Find all functions $f : \mathbb{R} \to \mathbb{R}$ such that for all real numbers x and y,

$$(x + f(x)^2)f(y) = f(yf(x)) + xyf(x).$$

Problem 115 (*Baltic Way 2017, Problem 5*).
Find all functions $f : \mathbb{R} \to \mathbb{R}$ such that

$$f(x^2 y) = f(xy) + yf(f(x) + y)$$

for all real numbers x and y.

Problem 116 (*Saudi Arabia IMO TST, Day 1, Problem 2*).
Find all functions $f : \mathbb{R} \to \mathbb{R}$ such that

$$f(xf(y) - y) + f(xy - x) + f(x + y) = 2xy$$

for all $x, y \in \mathbb{R}$.

Problem 117 (*2018 Hong Kong, TST 2, Problem 3*).
Find all functions $f : \mathbb{R} \to \mathbb{R}$ such that

$$f(f(xy - x)) + f(x + y) = yf(x) + f(y)$$

for all real numbers x and y.

Problem 118.
If f, g are non-constant functions from reals to reals that satisfy

$$f(x + y) = f(x)g(y) + g(x)f(y)$$

and

$$g(x + y) = g(x)g(y) - f(x)f(y),$$

then find all values that $f(0)$ and $g(0)$ can take.

Problem 119 (*Hong Kong IMO TST 2 2018, Problem 3*).
Find all functions $f : \mathbb{R} \to \mathbb{R}$ such that

$$f(f(xy - x)) + f(x + y) = yf(x) + f(y)$$

for all real numbers x and y.

Problem 120 (*Middle European Mathematical Olympiad 2017*).
Determine all functions $f : \mathbb{R} \to \mathbb{R}$ satisfying

$$f(x^2 + f(x)f(y)) = xf(x + y)$$

for all real numbers x and y.

Problem 121.
Find all functions $f : \mathbb{R} \to \mathbb{R}$ such that for any real numbers x and y,

$$f(yf(x) - xy - x) = f(x)f(y) - xf(y) + x.$$

Problem 122 (*IMO 2017, Problem 2 – Proposed by Dorlir Ahmeti, Albania*).
Let $\mathbb{R}$ be the set of real numbers. Determine all functions $f : \mathbb{R} \to \mathbb{R}$ such that, for any real numbers x and y,

$$f(f(x)f(y)) + f(x + y) = f(xy).$$

Problem 123 (*Canada Repêchage 2017, Problem 3*).
Determine all functions $f : \mathbb{R} \to \mathbb{R}$ that satisfy the following equation for all $x, y \in \mathbb{R}$:

$$(x + y)f(x - y) = f(x^2 - y^2).$$

Problem 124.
Find all functions $f : \mathbb{R} \to \mathbb{R}$ such that

$$f(f(x))f(y) - xy = f(x) + f(f(y)) - 1$$

holds for all reals x and y.

Problem 125 (*Harvard-MIT Mathematics Tournament 2017*).
Let $f : \mathbb{R} \to \mathbb{R}$ be a function satisfying $f(x)f(y) = f(x-y)$. Find all possible values of $f(2017)$.

Problem 126 (*India Postal Set 3, P2, 2016*).
Determine all functions $f : \mathbb{R} \to \mathbb{R}$ such that for all $x, y \in \mathbb{R}$

$$f(xf(y) - yf(x)) = f(xy) - xy.$$

Problem 127.
Find all functions $f : \mathbb{R} \to \mathbb{R}$ which satisfy

$$f(x^3) + f(y^3) + f(z^3) = (x + y + z)(f^2(x) + f^2(y) + f^2(z) - xy - yz - zx)$$

for all reals x, y, z.

Problem 128 (Estonia Open Contest 2017, Seniors, Problem O11).
Find all functions $f : \mathbb{R} \to \mathbb{R}$ such that for all reals x and y, we have

$$f(x + y)f(xy) = f(x^2 - y^2 + 1).$$

Problem 129 (Mongolia National Mathematical Olympiad 2017, Grade 12, Problem 1).
Find all functions $f : \mathbb{R} \to \mathbb{R}$ satisfying

$$(a - b)f(a + b) + (b - c)f(b + c) + (c - a)f(c + a) = 0$$

for all $a, b, c \in \mathbb{R}$.

Problem 130 (*Switzerland 2014, Problem 3*).
Find all functions $f : \mathbb{R} \to \mathbb{R}$ such that for all $x, y \in \mathbb{R}$:

$$f(x^2) + f(xy) = f(x)f(y) + yf(x) + xf(x + y).$$

Problem 131.
Find all functions $f : \mathbb{R} \to \mathbb{R}$ such that

$$f(f(x) + y) = f(x^2 - y) + 4yf(x), \quad \forall x, y \in \mathbb{R}.$$

Problem 132 (*IMO Shortlist 1997, Q22*).

Does there exist functions $f, g : \mathbb{R} \to \mathbb{R}$ such that $f(g(x)) = x^2$ and $g(f(x)) = x^k$ for all real numbers x

a) if $k = 3$?

b) if $k = 4$?

3.3 Functions Over $\mathbb{Q}$

3.3.1 Cauchy-type and Jensen-type

Problem 133.
Find all functions $f : \mathbb{Q} \setminus \{0\} \to \mathbb{Q}$ for which

$$f(m+n) = \frac{1}{f\left(\frac{1}{m}\right) + f\left(\frac{1}{n}\right)}$$

holds for any $m, n \in \mathbb{Q}$.

Problem 134.
Find all functions $f : \mathbb{Q} \to \mathbb{R} \setminus \{0\}$ such that

$$(f(x))^2 f(2y) + (f(y))^2 f(2x) = 2f(x)f(y)f(x+y)$$

for all $x, y \in \mathbb{Q}$.

3.3.2 Injective, Surjective, and Monotone Functions

Problem 135.
For any function $f : \mathbb{Q}^+ \to \mathbb{Q}$ satisfying

$$f(xy) = f(x) + f(y)$$

for all $x, y \in \mathbb{Q}^+$, prove that f is not injective. Also, prove that f can be surjective.

3.3.3 Functions on $\mathbb{Q}^+$

Problem 136.
Find all $f : \mathbb{Q}^+ \to \mathbb{Q}^+$ such that $f(x+1) = f(x)$ and

$$f\left(\frac{1}{x}\right) = x^2 f(x)$$

for all positive rational numbers x.

Problem 137 (*Benelux Mathematical Olympiad 2017, Problem 1*).
Find all functions $f : \mathbb{Q}^+ \to \mathbb{N}$ such that

$$f(xy) \cdot \gcd\left(f(x)f(y), f\left(\frac{1}{x}\right) f\left(\frac{1}{y}\right)\right) = xyf\left(\frac{1}{x}\right) f\left(\frac{1}{y}\right),$$

for all $x, y \in \mathbb{Q}^+$.

3.3.4   Miscellaneous

Problem 138.
Find all functions $f : \mathbb{Q} \to \mathbb{R}$ such that

$$f(x + y) + f(x - y) = 2 \max(f(x), f(y))$$

for all rationals x, y.

Problem 139 (*BDMO Regional Round 2017*).
Let $f : \mathbb{Q} \to \mathbb{R}$ be a function such that for all rationals x and y,

$$f(x + y) = f(x)f(y) - f(xy) + 1.$$

Suppose that $f(2017) \neq f(2018)$ and

$$f\left(\frac{2017}{2018}\right) = \frac{a}{b},$$

where a and b are coprime integers. What is $a + b$? Verify your answer.

Problem 140 (*Israel 2017*).
Let $f : \mathbb{Q} \times \mathbb{Q} \to \mathbb{Q}$ be a function satisfying:

1. For any $x_1, x_2, y_1, y_2 \in \mathbb{Q}$,

$$f\left(\frac{x_1 + x_2}{2}, \frac{y_1 + y_2}{2}\right) \leq \frac{f(x_1, y_1) + f(x_2, y_2)}{2}.$$

2. $f(0, 0) \leq 0$.

3. For any $x, y \in \mathbb{Q}$ satisfying $x^2 + y^2 > 100$, the inequality $f(x, y) > 1$ holds.

Prove that there is some positive rational number b such that for all rationals x, y,

$$f(x, y) \geq b\sqrt{x^2 + y^2} - \frac{1}{b}.$$

3.4 Functions Over $\mathbb{Z}$

3.4.1 Number Theoretic Functions

Problem 141.
Determine whether there exists a function $f : \mathbb{Z} \to \mathbb{N} \cup \{0\}$ such that $f(0) > 0$ and for each integer k, $f(k)$ is minimal value of $f(k-l) + f(l)$, where l ranges over all integers.

Problem 142.
Determine all functions $f : \mathbb{N} \to \mathbb{N}$ such that

$$\mathrm{lcm}(f(a), b) = \mathrm{lcm}(a, f(b))$$

for all natural numbers a and b.

Problem 143.
Find all functions $f, g : \mathbb{Q}^+ \to \mathbb{N}$ such that

$$f(xy) \cdot \gcd\left(f(x)f\left(\frac{1}{y}\right), f\left(\frac{1}{x}\right)f(y)\right) = xy \cdot g(xy) \cdot \mathrm{lcm}(f(x), f(y)),$$

for all $x, y \in \mathbb{Q}^+$.

Problem 144.
Find all functions $f : \mathbb{N} \to \mathbb{N}$ such that

$$xf(x) + yf(y) | (x^2 + y^2)^{2018}$$

for all positive integers m, n.

Problem 145 (*Japan Mathematical Olympiad Finals 2018, Problem 5*).
Let T be a positive integer. Find all functions $f : \mathbb{N} \times \mathbb{N} \to \mathbb{N}$ for which there exist integers $C_0, C_1, \ldots, C_T$ satisfying:

1. For any positive integer n, the number of positive integer pairs (k, l) such that $f(k, l) = n$ is exactly n.

2. For any $t = 0, 1, \ldots, T$, as well as for any positive integer pair (k, l), the equality
$$f(k + t, l + T - t) - f(k, l) = C_t$$
holds.

Problem 146 (*Japan Mathematical Olympiad Finals 2018, Problem 3*).
Let $S = \{1, 2, \ldots, 999\}$. Consider a function $f : S \to S$, such that for any $n \in S$,
$$f^{n+f(n)+1}(n) = f^{nf(n)}(n) = n.$$
Prove that there exists $a \in S$, such that $f(a) = a$. Here $f^k(n)$ is k times composition of f with itself.

Problem 147 (*Indian National Mathematical Olympiad 2018, Turkey IMO TST 2016*).
Let $f : \mathbb{N} \to \mathbb{N}$ be a function such that $f(mn) = f(m)f(n)$ and
$$m + n \text{ divides } f(m) + f(n)$$
for all $m, n \in \mathbb{N}$. Prove that there exists an odd natural number k such that $f(n) = n^k$ for all n in $\mathbb{N}$.

Problem 148.
Find all multiplicative functions $f : \mathbb{N} \to \mathbb{R}$ such that
$$f(n+] = f(n)$$
for all positive integers n.

Problem 149 (*China Mathematical Olympiad 2018, Problem 1*).
Let n be a positive integer. Let A_n denote the set of primes p such that there exists positive integers a, b satisfying
$$\frac{a + b}{p} \text{ and } \frac{a^n + b^n}{p^2}$$
are both integers that are relatively prime to p. If A_n is finite, let $f(n)$ denote $|A_n|$.

a) Prove that A_n is finite if and only if $n \neq 2$.

b) Let m, k be odd positive integers and let d be their greatest common divisor. Show that
$$f(d) \leq f(k) + f(m) - f(km) \leq 2f(d).$$

Problem 150 (*Balkan 2017, Problem 3 – Proposed by Dorlir Ahmeti, Albania*).
Find all functions $f : \mathbb{N} \to \mathbb{N}$ such that
$$n + f(m) \text{ divides } f(n) + nf(m)$$
for all $m, n \in \mathbb{N}$.

Problem 151 (*IMO Shortlist 2016, Croatia IMO TST 2017 Problem 4 – Proposed by Dorlir Ahmeti, Albania*).
Find all functions $f : \mathbb{N} \to \mathbb{N}$ such that for all positive integers a and b,

$$f(a) + f(b) - ab \mid af(a) + bf(b).$$

Problem 152 (*Serbia IMO TST 2017, Problem 3 – Proposed by Marko Radovanović*).
Call a function $f : \mathbb{N} \to \mathbb{N}$ *lively* if

$$f(a + b - 1) = f^a(b)$$

for all positive integers a and b, where f^a is a times composition of f with itself. Suppose that g is a lively function such that $g(A+] = g(A) + 1$ holds for some $A \geq 2$.

(a) Prove that
$$g\left(n + 2017^{2017}\right) = g(n)$$

for all $n \geq A + 2$.

(b) If
$$g\left(A + 2017^{2017}\right) \neq g(A)$$

, determine $g(n)$ for $n \leq A - 1$.

Problem 153 (*Canadian Mathematical Olympiad 2017*).
Define a function $f : \mathbb{N} \to \mathbb{N}$ such that $f(f(n))$ is the number of positive integer divisors of n. Prove that if p is a prime, then $f(p)$ is prime.

Problem 154 (*Harvard-MIT Mathematics Tournament 2017 – Proposed by Yang Liu*).
Compute the number of functions $f : \mathbb{N} \to \{0, 1, \ldots, 16\}$ such that

$$f(x + 17) = f(x) \qquad \text{and} \qquad f(x^2) \equiv f(x)^2 + 15 \pmod{17}$$

for all integers $x \geq 1$.

Problem 155 (*Turkey IMO TST 2016, Problem 5 – Proposed by Melih Üçer*).
Find all functions $f : \mathbb{N} \to \mathbb{N}$ such that for all $m, n \in \mathbb{N}$ we have $f(mn) = f(m)f(n)$ and $m + n \mid f(m) + f(n)$.

3.4.2   Functions on $\mathbb{N}$

Problem 156 (*Closely related to IMO 1992, Problem 2 – Taken from [1]*).
Find all functions $f : \mathbb{N} \to \mathbb{N}$ such that

$$f(m^2 + f(n)) = f(m)^2 + n$$

for all $m, n \in \mathbb{N}$.

Problem 157.
Find all functions $f : \mathbb{N} \to \mathbb{N}$ such tat $f(1) > 0$ and

$$f(m^2 + n^2) = f(m)^2 + f(n)^2$$

holds for all $m, n \in \mathbb{N} \cup \{0\}$.

Problem 158 (*CIP alert*).
Let k be a fixed positive integer. Find all functions $f : \mathbb{N} \to \mathbb{N}$ such that

$$f(m + f(n)) + f(n + f(m))|2(m + n)^k$$

hold for all integers $m, n \geq 1$.

Problem 159 (*CIP alert*).
Find all functions $f : \mathbb{N} \to \mathbb{R}$ such that

$$f(n) = f(n^2 + n + 1)$$

for any $n \in \mathbb{N}$.

Problem 160.
Prove that there exist infinitely many functions $f : \mathbb{N} \to \mathbb{N}$ such that

$$f(x)^2 = f(2x) + 2f(x) - 2, \quad \forall x \in \mathbb{N}, \quad \text{and} \quad f(1) = 3.$$

Problem 161 (*Macedonia National Olympiad 2017, Problem 1*).
Find all functions $f : \mathbb{N} \to \mathbb{N}$ such that for each natural integer $n > 1$ and
for all $x, y \in \mathbb{N}$ the following holds:

$$f(x + y) = f(x) + f(y) + \sum_{k=1}^{n-1} \binom{n}{k} x^{n-k} y^k.$$

Problem 162.
Find all functions $f : \mathbb{N} \to \mathbb{N}$ such that $f(1) = 1$ and

$$f(a + b + ab) = a + b + f(ab)$$

for all positive integers a and b.

3.4.3   Trigonometric and Periodic Functions

Problem 163 (*China TST 2018, Day 2, Problem 1*).
Functions $f, g : \mathbb{Z} \to \mathbb{Z}$ satisfy

$$f(g(x) + y) = g(f(y) + x)$$

for any integers x, y. If f is bounded, prove that g is periodic.

3.4.4   Inequalities

Problem 164.
How many functions

$$f : \{1, 2, 3, \ldots, n\} \to \{1, 2, 3, \ldots, n\}$$

can be defined such that $f(1) < f(2) < f(3)$?

Problem 165 (*European Mathematical Cup 2017, Seniors, Problem 1 – Proposed by Adrian Beker*).
Find all functions $f : \mathbb{N} \to \mathbb{N}$ such that

$$f(x) + yf(f(x)) \leq x(1 + f(y))$$

for all positive integers x and y.

Problem 166 (*Final Korean Mathematical Olympiad 2017, Day 1, Problem 3*).
For a positive integer n, denote $c_n = 2017^n$. A function $f : \mathbb{N} \to \mathbb{R}$ satisfies the following two conditions:

1. For all positive integers m, n,

$$f(m + n) \leq 2017 \cdot f(m) \cdot f(n + 325).$$

2. For all positive integers n, we have

$$0 < f(c_{n+1}) < f(c_n)^{2017}.$$

Prove that there exists a sequence $\{a_n\}_{n=1}^{\infty}$ which satisfies the following: for all n, k such that $a_k < n$, we have

$$f(n)^{c_k} < f(c_k)^n.$$

Problem 167 (*Korea Winter Program Practice 2017, Test 1, Day 2, Problem 1*).
Let $f : \mathbb{Z} \to \mathbb{R}$ be a function satisfying $f(x) + f(y) + f(z) \geq 0$ for all integers x, y, z with $x + y + z = 0$. Prove that

$$f(-2017) + f(-2016) + \cdots + f(2016) + f(2017) \geq 0.$$

Problem 168.
Determine the number of increasing functions $f : (1, 2, \ldots, m) \to (1, 2, \ldots, m)$ for which $|f(x) - f(y)| \leq |x - y|$, where $m \in \mathbb{N}$.

Problem 169.
Find all surjective functions $f : \mathbb{N} \to \mathbb{N}$ such that $f(n) \geq n + (-1)^n$ holds for all $n \in \mathbb{N}$.

Problem 170 (*Singapore Mathematical Olympiad 2017, Senior Section, Round 2, Problem 4*).
Find all functions $f : \mathbb{N} \to \mathbb{N}$ such that $f(k + 1) > f(f(k))$ for all $k \geq 1$.

3.4.5   Miscellaneous

Substitutions

Problem 171.
The function f is defined on non negative integers by $f(0) = 0$ and $f(2n + 1) = 2f(n)$ for $n \geq 0$ and $f(2n) = 2f(n) + 1$ for $n \geq 1$. Show that if $g(n) = f(f(n))$, then $g(n - g(n)) = 0$ for any $n \geq 0$.

Problem 172.
Find all functions $f : \mathbb{Z} \to \mathbb{Z}$ satisfying

$$f(x + f(y)) = f(x)$$

for all integers x, y.

Problem 173 (*European Girls' Mathematical Olympiad 2017, Day 1, Problem 2*).
Find the smallest positive integer k for which there exists a colouring of the positive integers $\mathbb{N}$ with k colours and a function $f : \mathbb{N} \to \mathbb{N}$ with the following two properties:

(i) For all positive integers m, n of the same colour, $f(m + n) = f(m) + f(n)$.

(ii) There are positive integers m, n such that $f(m+n) \neq f(m) + f(n)$.

Note. In a colouring of $\mathbb{N}$ with k colours, every integer is coloured in exactly one of the k colours. In both (i) and (ii) the positive integers m, n are not necessarily distinct.

Problem 174 (*Macedonia National Olympiad 2017, Problem 5*).
Let $n > 1$ be an integer and suppose that $a_1, a_2, \ldots, a_n$ is a sequence of n natural integers. Define the sequence $\{b_i\}$ by

$$b_1 = \left\lfloor \frac{a_2 + \cdots + a_n}{n-1} \right\rfloor,$$

$$b_i = \left\lfloor \frac{a_1 + \cdots + a_{i-1} + a_{i+1} + \cdots + a_n}{n-1} \right\rfloor, \quad \text{for} \quad i = 2, \ldots, n-1,$$

$$b_n = \left\lfloor \frac{a_1 + \cdots + a_{n-1}}{n-1} \right\rfloor.$$

Define a mapping f by

$$f(a_1, a_2, \ldots a_n) = (b_1, b_2, \ldots, b_n).$$

a) Let $g : \mathbb{N} \to \mathbb{N}$ be a function such that $g(1)$ is the number of different elements in $f(a_1, a_2, \cdots a_n)$ and $g(m)$ is the number od different elements in

$$f^m(a_1, a_2, \cdots a_n) = f(f^{m-1}(a_1, a_2, \cdots a_n)), \quad m > 1.$$

Prove that there exists $k_0 \in \mathbb{N}$ such that for $m \geq k_0$, the function $g(m)$ is periodic.

b) Prove that

$$\sum_{m=1}^{k} \frac{g(m)}{m(m+1)} < C, \quad \text{for all } k \in \mathbb{N},$$

where C is a function that doesn't depend on k.

Problem 175.
Find all functions $f : \mathbb{N} \to \mathbb{N} \cup \{0\}$ such that $f(f(n)) = f(n+1) - f(n)$ for all positive integers n.

Chapter 4

Selected Solutions

4.1 Functions Over $\mathbb{C}$

Problem 1. Let

$$f(x) = \begin{cases} z, & \text{if } \Re(z) \geq 0, \\ -z, & \text{if } \Re(z) < 0, \end{cases}$$

be a function defined on $\mathbb{C}$. A sequence $\{z_n\}$ is defined as $z_1 = u$ and for all $n \geq 1$,

$$z_{n+1} = f\left(z_n^2 + z_n + 1\right).$$

Given $\{z_n\}$ is periodic, find all possible values of u.

Solution (by pco). Note that $\Re(f(x)) \geq 0$ whatever x is, and so $\Re(z_n) \geq 0$ for all integers $n \geq 2$. Let $z_n = a + ib$ for some $n \geq 2$ (so that $a \geq 0$). Then,

$$z_n^2 + z_n + 1 = (a^2 - b^2 + a + 1) + i(2ab + b),$$

and therefore,

$$\begin{aligned} |z_n^2 + z_n + 1|^2 &= (a^2 - b^2 + a + 1)^2 + (2ab + b)^2 \\ &= a^2 + b^2 + (a^2 - b^2 + 1)^2 + 4a^2b^2 + 2a(a^2 + b^2 + 1) \\ &\geq a^2 + b^2. \end{aligned}$$

Since $|f(x)| = |x|$, we get

$$|z_{n+1}| \geq |z_n|, \quad \forall n \geq 2.$$

So, periodicity implies $|z_{n+1}| = |z_n|$ and thus $a = 0$ and $b = \pm 1$. Hence, $z_n = \pm i$ for all $n \geq 2$. This means that $u \in \{-i, +i\}$.

Problem 2. Consider the functional equation $af(z) + bf(w^2 z) = g(z)$, where w is a complex cube root of unity, a and b are fixed complex numbers, and $g(z)$ is a known complex function. Prove that the complex function $f(z)$ can be uniquely determined if $a^3 + b^3 \neq 0$

Solution (by pco). Note that

$$\begin{aligned} af(z) + bf(w^2 z) &= g(z), \\ af(wz) + bf(z) &= g(wz), \\ af(w^2 z) + bf(wz) &= g(w^2 z). \end{aligned}$$

If $a = 0$ and $b \neq 0$, first equation uniquely defines $f(z)$. If $a \neq 0$ and $b = 0$, then the first equation uniquely defines $f(z)$. Finally, if $ab \neq 0$, it is easy to cancel $f(wz)$ and $f(w^2 z)$ amongst the three equations and we get

$$(a^3 + b^3)f(z) = \text{some expression not depending on } f.$$

4.2   Functions Over $\mathbb{R}$

4.2.1   Cauchy-type and Jensen-type

Problem 4. Find all functions $f : \mathbb{R} \to \mathbb{R}$ such that for any $x, y \in \mathbb{R}$,

$$f(x) + f(x + f(y)) = y + f(f(x) + f(f(y))).$$

Solution (by pco). Let $P(x, y)$ be the given assertion. Let $a = f(0)$ and $b = f(a)$. Subtracting $P(f(x), 0)$ from $P(a, x)$, we get $f(f(x)) = b - x$. Note that this implies that $f(x)$ is bijective. Then $P(f(x), y)$ implies

$$f(f(x) + f(y)) = x + y - b + f(2b - x - y).$$

And $P(a, x + y)$ implies

$$f(f(0) + f(x + y)) = x + y - b + f(2b - x - y).$$

And so, since f is injective, $f(x + y) + a = f(x) + f(y)$ and $f(x) - a$ is additive. Using this additivity back in original equation, it is easy to show that no such function satisfies the given condition.

Problem 6. Find all functions $f : \mathbb{R} \to \mathbb{R}$ such that for some $a, b \in \mathbb{R}$,

$$f(x)f(y) = x^a f\left(\frac{y}{2}\right) + y^b f\left(\frac{x}{2}\right)$$

holds for all reals x and y.

Solution (by TuZo). If $a = b$, we can denote

$$\frac{f(x)}{x^a} = g(x),$$

so that

$$g(x)g(y) = g(x) + g(y), \quad \forall x, y \in \mathbb{R},$$

and here use the new function $h(x) = g(e^x)$ to get $h(x + y) = h(x) + h(y)$. This is the classic Cauchy equation with the solution $h(x) = kx$ for all real x and any real k.

Problem 7. Find all functions $f : \mathbb{R}^+ \to \mathbb{R}^+$ satisfying $f(xf(y)) = yf(x)$ for all positive reals x and y, and $\lim_{x \to \infty} f(x) = 0$.

Solution (by pco). Clearly, $f(x)$ is bijective: if $f(a) = f(b)$ then

$$bf(x) = f(xf(b)) = f(xf(a)) = af(x)$$

and so $a = b$. We also have

$$f\left(xf\left(\frac{y}{f(x)}\right)\right) = y$$

and so $f(x)$ is surjective. We have $f(xf(1)) = f(x)$ and so, since f is bijective, $f(1) = 1$. Plugging $x = 1$ and $y = t$ then gives $f(f(t)) = t$ for all positive t and so

$$f(xy) = f(xf(f(y))) = f(x)f(y), \quad \forall x, y \in \mathbb{R}^+.$$

Setting then $f(x) = e^{g(\ln x)}$, we get

$$g(x + y) = g(x) + g(y), \quad \forall x, y \in \mathbb{R}.$$

Now, $\lim_{x \to +\infty} g(x) = -\infty$ and so $g(x)$ is upperbounded from a given point and so is linear. Plugging this back in original equation, we get $g(x) = -x$ and so

$$f(x) = \frac{1}{x}, \quad \forall x > 0.$$

4.2.2   Continuity

Problem 9. Find all continuous functions $f : \mathbb{R} \to \mathbb{R}$ such that

$$f(x + y)f(x - y) = (f(x)f(y))^2, \quad \forall x, y \in \mathbb{R}.$$

Solution (by pco). Let $P(x, y)$ be the assertion

$$f(x + y)f(x - y) = f(x)^2 f(y)^2.$$

$P(0, 0)$ gives us $f(0) \in \{-1, 0, 1\}$. So, we break the problem into two cases.

1. If $f(0) = 0$, then $P(x, 0)$ implies $f \equiv 0$, which is indeed a solution.

2. If $f(0) \neq 0$, then $f(x)$ being a solution implies $-f(x)$ is a solution too. So, WLOG, suppose that $f(0) = 1$. If $f(a) = 0$ for some a, then

$$P\left(\frac{a}{2}, \frac{a}{2}\right) \implies f\left(\frac{a}{2}\right) = 0$$

$$\implies f\left(\frac{a}{2n}\right) = 0, \quad \forall n \in \mathbb{N}.$$

Continuity would then imply $f(0) = 0$. So, no such a exists and we have $f(x) > 0$ for all real x. Let then $g(x) = \ln f(x)$ so that functional equation becomes a new assertion $Q(x, y)$:

$$g(x + y) + g(x - y) = 2g(x) + 2g(y),$$

where g is continuous and $g(0) = 0$. Now,

$$Q(0, x) \implies g(-x) = g(x),$$
$$Q(x, x) \implies g(2x) = 4g(x),$$
$$Q(2x, x) \implies g(3x) = 9g(x).$$

Easy induction on n for $Q(nx, x)$ gives

$$g(nx) = n^2 g(x), \quad \forall x \in \mathbb{R}, n \in \mathbb{N}.$$

From there we easily get $g(x) = x^2 g(1)$ for all rational x and continuity allows us to conclude that $g(x) = cx^2$. Hence, $f(x) = e^{cx^2}$ for any real c, and one can easily check that this is indeed a solution. Since we assumed $f(0) = 1$ in the beginning, we must also consider the other solution $f(x) = -e^{cx^2}$.

Problem 11. Find all continuous functions $f : \mathbb{R} \to \mathbb{R}$ such that:

$$f(x - f(y)) = f(x) - y$$

for all real numbers x, y.

Solution (by pco). Let $P(x, y)$ be the given assertion.

$$P(f(x), x) \implies f(f(x)) = x + f(0),$$

and so $f(x)$ is bijective. Let then u such that $f(u) = 0$.

$$P(x, u) \implies u = 0,$$

and so $f(0) = 0$. Therefore, $f(f(x)) = x$. Now, $P(x + y, f(y))$ implies that $f(x+y) = f(x)+f(y)$. It is now easy to conclude that problem is equivalent to find all involutive (functions with $f(f(x)) = x$) and additive functions. Now, because of continuity, additivity implies linearity and involutivity implies two solutions: $f(x) = x$ and $f(x) = -x$ for all x.

Problem 13. Find all continuous functions $f : \mathbb{R} \to \mathbb{R}$ such that

$$f(xy) + f(x + y) = f(xy + x) + f(y)$$

for all real numbers x, y.

Solution (by pco). Let $P(x, y)$ be the given assertion and let $c = f(1)$ and $d = f(-1)$. Note that if $f(x)$ is a solution then $f(x) + c$ is also a solution. So, WLOG, assume that $f(0) = 0$. Let $a, b > 0$ and define the sequences $\{x_n\}$ and $\{y_n\}$ recursively so that $x_1 = a$ and $y_1 = b$ and

$$x_{n+1} = \frac{x_n}{y_n + 1} \quad \text{and} \quad y_{n+1} = \frac{(x_n + y_n + 1)y_n}{y_n + 1}$$

for all $n \geq 1$. It is easy to show that

$$\lim_{n \to +\infty} = 0 \quad \text{and} \quad \lim_{n \to +\infty} y_n = a + b.$$

Subtracting $P(x_n/y_n + 1, y_n)$ from $P(y_n, x_n/y_n + 1)$, we get

$$f(x_n) + f(y_n) = f(x_{n+1}) + f(y_{n+1}),$$

and so, setting $n \to +\infty$ and using continuity,

$$f(a) + f(b) = f(a + b).$$

And so, since f is continuous,

$$f(x) = cx, \quad \forall x \geq 0.$$

Let then $x \leq -1$. In this case, $P(-x, -1)$ implies $f(x) = cx + c + d$ for all $x \leq -1$. Let then $x \in (-1, 0)$ and choose $y > \max(-x, -\frac{1}{x})$ so that $y(x + 1) > 0$, $x + y > 0$, and $xy < -1$.

$$P(y, x) \implies f(x) = cx + c + d, \quad \forall x \in (-1, 0).$$

Continuity at 0 gives $c + d = 0$ and so $f(x) = cx$, which indeed is a solution. Hence the general solution is $f(x) = ax + b$, $\forall x$ which indeed is a solution, whatever are $a, b \in \mathbb{R}$.

4.2.3 Injective, Surjective, and Monotone Functions

Problem 18. Find all monotone functions $f : \mathbb{R} \to \mathbb{R}$ such that $f(2018x) = f(x) + 2017x$ for all real numbers x.

Solution (by pco). Let

$$a = \lim_{x \to 0+} f(x) \text{ and } b = \lim_{x \to 0-} f(x)$$

(which exist since f is monotonous). Easy induction implies

$$f(2018^n x) = f(x) + (2018^n - 1)x, \quad \forall x \in \mathbb{R}, \forall n \in \mathbb{Z}.$$

- If $x > 0$, set $n \to -\infty$ to get $f(x) = x + a, \forall x > 0$.

- If $x < 0$ set $n \to -\infty$ to get $f(x) = x + b, \forall x < 0$.

Hence the solution is

$$f(x) = x + a, \quad \forall x < 0, \text{ and } f(0) = c, \text{ and } f(x) = x + b, \quad \forall x > 0$$

This indeed is a solution for any choice of a, b, and c with $a \leq c \leq b$.

Problem 20. Let $f : \mathbb{R} \to \mathbb{R}$ be a function such that

$$f(a + 2f(a)f(b)) = f(a) + 2af(b)$$

for all reals a and b. Also, suppose that f is not the all-zero function.

1. Prove that f is surjective.

2. Find all such f.

Solution (by pco).

1. Let $P(x, y)$ be the assertion

$$f(x + 2f(x)f(y)) = f(x) + 2xf(y)$$

and let u, v be reals such that $f(u) = v \neq 0$. Let $A = f(\mathbb{R})$.

If $f(t) = 0$ for some t; then $P(t, u)$ gives $t = 0$ and so $f(0) = 0$ (if such t exists). Now,

$$P\left(-\frac{1}{2}, -\frac{1}{2}\right) \implies f\left(-\frac{1}{2} + 2f(-\frac{1}{2})^2\right) = 0,$$

and so $f(-1/2)^2 = 1/4$. If f is a solution, then $-f$ is a solution. So, WLOG, assume that $f(-1/2) = -1/2$ and $f(0) = 0$. Then,

$$P\left(-\frac{1}{2}, x\right) \implies f\left(-\frac{1}{2} - f(x)\right) = -\frac{1}{2} - f(x),$$

$$P\left(-\frac{1}{2}, -\frac{1}{2} - f(x)\right) \implies f(f(x)) = f(x),$$

$$P\left(f(x), -\frac{1}{2} - f(y)\right) \implies f(-2f(x)f(y)) = -2f(x)f(y).$$

So $a, b \in A$ implies $-2ab \in A$ and $a, b, c, d \in A$ implies $-8abcd \in A$. Take any $a \neq 0 \in A$. We have

$$P\left(\frac{1}{4a}, -2f(x)a\right) \implies f\left(\frac{1}{4a} - 4f\left(\frac{1}{4a}\right)^2 a\right) = 0.$$

Therefore, $f(1/(4a))^2 = 1/(16a^2)$ and so

$$\frac{\epsilon(a)}{4a} \in A \text{ for some } \epsilon(a) \in \{-1, +1\}.$$

Choosing

$$(a, b, c, d) \mapsto \left(\frac{\epsilon(a)}{4a}, \frac{\epsilon(a)}{4a}, a, b\right),$$

since $-8abcd \in A$, we find that

$$-\frac{b}{2a} \in A \text{ for all } a \neq 0 \in A \text{ and } b \in A.$$

Now, $P(x, -2f(x)f(u))$ yields $f(x - 4f(x)^2v) = f(x)(1 - 4xv)$, and so

$$\frac{f(x - 4f(x)^2v)}{f(x)} = 1 - 4xv, \quad \forall x \neq 0.$$

Thus, $\frac{b}{a}$ (with $a, b \in A$, $a \neq 0$) can take any value we want. Combining with the fact that $-b/2a \in A$, we get that $f(x)$ is surjective.

2. Since we previously got $f(f(x)) = f(x)$, surjectivity then implies that $f(x) = x$ for all x, which is indeed a solution. We should not forget about the other solution $f(x) = -x$ for all x (this is because if f is a solution, then so is $-f$). The latter solution also satisfies the original equation and hence is a valid solution.

Problem 21. In each of the following parts, if $f : \mathbb{R}^+ \to \mathbb{R}^+$ is a function that satisfies the given condition for all positive reals x and y, show that f is injecive.

1. $f(f(x) + f(y)) = f(2x) - f(x) + f(2y) - y$.

2. $f(f(3x) + 3f(y)) = x + 2f(x) + f(3y)$.

3. $f(3xy) = 2f(xy) + xf(y)$.

4. $f(3x + f(y)) = f(2x) + x + 2f(y) - y$.

5. $f(x + 2f(x) + f(3y)) = 3f(x) + y + 2f(y)$.

Solution (by pco).

1. Subtract $P(x, 1)$ from $P(1, x)$.

2. If $f(a) = f(b)$, then comparing $P(1, a)$ with $P(1, b)$, we get $f(3a) = f(3b)$ and comparing $P(a, 1)$ with $P(b, 1)$, we get $a + 2f(a) = b + 2f(b)$. So $a = b$.

3. Subtract $P(1, 1)$ from $P(1/x, x)$.

4. Subtract $P(1, a)$ from $P(1, b)$.

5. Let $P(x, y)$ be the assertion $f(x + 2f(x) + f(3y)) = 3f(x) + y + 2f(y)$. Suppose that $f(3a) = f(3b)$ for some positive reals a and b. Comparing $P(1, a)$ with $P(1, b)$, we get $a + 2f(a) = b + 2f(b)$. Comparing $P(a, 1)$ with $P(b, 1)$, we get $f(a) = f(b)$. Hence, $a = b$ and so $3a = 3b$. This means that f is injective.

Problem 22. Find all surjective functions $f : \mathbb{R} \to \mathbb{R}$ such that

$$f(xf(y) + y^2) = f((x + y)^2) - xf(x)$$

for all real numbers x, y.

Solution (by talkon). Denote the given equation by $P(x, y)$. Then, $P(f(y) - 2y, y)$ gives, for all $y \in \mathbb{R}$,

$$(f(y) - 2y)f(f(y) - 2y)) = 0.$$

Hence for all $y \in \mathbb{R}$, either $f(y) = 2y$ or $f(f(y) - 2y) = 0$. Now we consider the set of roots of f, denoted by A. These are the relevant properties of A:

1. If $a \in A$ then Since $f(a) = 0 \neq 2a$, $f(f(a) - 2a) = 0$ so $-2a \in A$.

2. If $a, b \in A$, from $P(a, b)$, $P(b, a)$ we have $f(a^2) = f((a + b)^2) = f(b^2)$.

3. If $a, b \in A$, comparing $P(x - a, a)$ and $P(x - a, b)$ gives $f(x^2) = f((x + a - b)^2)$ for all x.

4. If $a, b \in A$, $P(b - a, a)$ gives $b - a \in A$.

Suppose that A contains a nonzero element u. Setting $(a, b) = (u, -2u)$ in 3 gives us $f(x^2) = f((x + 3u)^2)$ for all x. Also, from 4 we have $u - (-2u) = 3u \in A$. Comparing $P(x, 0)$ and $P(x, 3u)$ gives

$$f(xf(0)) = f(9u^2).$$

If $f(0) \neq 0$ then it follows that f is constant, which is a contradiction, so $f(0) = 0$.

Now $P(x, 0)$ gives $xf(x) = x^2$ for all $x \in \mathbb{R}$, hence we can rewrite the original equation as

$$f(xf(y) + y^2) = f((x + y)^2) - f(x^2).$$

Now setting x as $x + 3u$ in the above equation, then comparing, gives

$$f((x + 3u)f(y) + y^2) = f(xf(y) + y^2)$$

for all $x, y \in \mathbb{R}$.

Finally, setting $x = -\frac{y^2}{f(y)}$ gives $f(3uf(y)) = f(0)$ for all $y \in \mathbb{R}$ such that $f(y) \neq 0$. However, f is surjective, so $3uf(y)$ is surjective, so f must be constant, which is a contradiction. Therefore A cannot contain a nonzero element.

Now if f is not the function $x \mapsto 2x$ then, for some x_0, we have $f(x_0) \neq 2x_0$, which implies $f(x_0) - 2x_0 \in A$, which is impossible.

Therefore, the function $f(x) = 2x$ for all x is the only solution.

Problem 25. Find all functions $f : \mathbb{R} \to \mathbb{R}$ satisfying the relation

$$f(xf(y) - f(x)) = 2f(x) + xy$$

for all $x, y \in \mathbb{R}$.

Solution (by ThE-dArK-lOrD). As usual, let $P(x, y)$ denote the assertion

$$f(xf(y) - f(x)) = 2f(x) + xy, \quad \forall x, y \in \mathbb{R}.$$

$P(1, y)$ gives us $f(f(y) - f(1)) = 2f(1) + y$ for all $y \in \mathbb{R}$, so f is surjective. If $t \in \mathbb{R}$ is such that $f(t) = 0$, then $P(t, t)$ implies $f(0) = t^2$ and $P(t, 0)$ implies $f(tf(0)) = 0$. Hence, $f(0) = (tf(0))^2$. This immediately implies So $f(0) = f(0)^3$ and so $f(0) \in \{0, 1, -1\}$.

1. If $f(0) = -1$, we get that $-1 = t^2$, which contradicts the t being a real number.

2. If $f(0) = 0$, then $P(x, 0)$ gives us $f(-f(x)) = 2f(x)$ for all $x \in \mathbb{R}$, and by surjectivity, $f(-x) = 2x$ for all $x \in \mathbb{R}$, which is not a solution.

So, $f(0) = 1$. Now, $P(0, 0)$ implies $f(-1) = 2$ and $P(1, 1)$ gives $f(1) = 0$. Then, using $P(1, x)$, one can find that $f(2) = -1$. By $P(x, 2)$,

$$f(-x - f(x)) = 2f(x) + 2x, \quad \text{for all } x \in \mathbb{R}.$$

For each $x \in \mathbb{R}$, let z be a real number such that $f(z) = x + f(x)$. Then, $P(z, 1)$ gives us

$$f(-f(z)) = 2f(z) + z = f(-x - f(x)) = 2f(x) + 2x = 2x + 2f(x) + z,$$

and thus $z = 0$. Finally, we get that $f(0) = 1 = x + f(x)$ for all $x \in \mathbb{R}$, which means $f(x) = 1 - x$ for all $x \in \mathbb{R}$.

Problem 26. Given real number $a \notin \{-1, 0, 1\}$, find all functions $f : \mathbb{R} \to \mathbb{R}$ such that

$$f(f(x) + ay) = (a^2 + a)x + f(f(y) - x)$$

for all reals x and y.

Solution (by pco). Let $P(x, y)$ be the given assertion and let $b = f(0)$. Since $a \neq 0$, $P(x, -\frac{f(x)}{a})$ implies

$$f(0) - (a^2 + a)x = f\left(f\left(-\frac{f(x)}{a}\right) - x\right).$$

Since $a^2 + a \neq 0$, LHS can take any value we want and so $f(x)$ is surjective. If $f(u) = f(v)$, subtracting $P(x, u)$ from $P(x, v)$ implies

$$f(f(x) + au) = f(f(x) + av)$$

and so, since f is surjective,

$$f(x + au) = f(x + av),$$

and so $f(x)$ is periodic with period $T = a(u - v)$. Subtracting then $P(x, y)$ from $P(x + T, y)$, we get $T = 0$ (since $a^2 + a \neq 0$) and so $f(x)$ is injective. Then $P(0, x)$ gives $f(f(x)) = f(ax + b)$ and so, since f is injective,

$$f(x) = ax + b, \quad \forall x \in \mathbb{R}$$

which indeed is a solution, whatever is $b \in \mathbb{R}$.

Problem 27. Find all functions $f : \mathbb{R} \to \mathbb{R}$ such that

$$f(f(x) - xf(y)) + xy = 2f(x)$$

for all $x, y \in \mathbb{R}$.

Solution (by pco). Let $P(x, y)$ be the assertion

$$f(f(x) - xf(y)) + xy = 2f(x).$$

Let $a = f(0)$ and define

$$T = \left\{ \frac{f(x)}{x} : x \in \mathbb{R} \setminus \{0\} \right\}.$$

Note that $f(x) = 0$ for all $x \neq 0$ is not a solution and so there exists $t_1 \in T$ such that $t_1 \neq 0$. Now,

$$P(1, x) \implies f(f(1) - f(x)) = 2f(1) - x,$$

and so f is bijective. Take any $x \neq 0$. Then, $P(x, f(x)/x)$ implies (using injectivity) that $f(t) = t - 1$ holds for all $t \in T$. This means that

$$t_2 = \frac{f(t_1)}{t_1} = 1 - \frac{1}{t_1} \in T.$$

(Note that $t_2 \neq t_1$). Consider any $x \neq 0$ and $t \in T$. Since $f(x)$ is surjective, there exists some y such that $f(y) = \frac{f(x) - t}{x}$. Then, for this choice of y,

$$P(x, y) \implies y = \frac{2f(x) + 1 - t}{x},$$

and so

$$f\left(\frac{2f(x) + 1 - t}{x}\right) = \frac{f(x) - t}{x}, \quad \forall x \neq 0 \text{ and } \forall t \in T.$$

If $f(x) \neq (t-1)/2$, this gives

$$\frac{f(x) - t}{2f(x) + 1 - t} \in T.$$

But $f(x)$ being surjective means that $\frac{f(x)-t}{2f(x)+1-t}$ can take any real value except

$$\frac{1}{2} \quad \text{and} \quad \frac{a - t}{2a + 1 - t}.$$

The exclusion of $\frac{a-t}{2a+1-t}$ (which needs $x = 0$) is easy to discard using either t_1 or t_2. And so, we get that $f(x) = x - 1$ holds for all $x \neq 1/2$. Then,

$$P\left(\frac{3}{2}, 1\right) \implies f\left(\frac{1}{2}\right) = -\frac{1}{2}.$$

Therefore, $f(x) = x - 1$ for all real x. One can check that this is indeed a valid solution.

Problem 28. Find all functions $f, g : \mathbb{R} \to \mathbb{R}$ such that

$$f(x - 3f(y)) = xf(y) - yf(x) + g(x), \quad \forall x, y \in \mathbb{R},$$

and $g(1) = -8$.

Solution (by pco). Let $P(x, y)$ be the assertion

$$f(x - 3f(y)) = xf(y) - yf(x) + g(x).$$

Let $a = f(0)$ and note that $f \equiv 0$ would imply $g \equiv 0$, which is impossible since $g(1) = -8$. So, there exist reals u, v such that $f(u) = v \neq 0$. Then, comparison of $P(u, x)$ with $P(u, y)$ implies $f(x)$ injective. If $a = 0$, $P(x, 0)$ implies $f(x) = g(x)$ and $P(x, x)$ implies $f(x - 3f(x)) = g(x)$. Therefore,

$$f(x) = f(x - 3f(x)),$$

and since f is injective, $f(x) = 0$; impossible.
    Thus, $a \neq 0$. Now, $P(0, x)$ gives

$$f(-3f(x)) = -ax + g(0),$$

and since $a \neq 0$, $f(x)$ is bijective. Let then, u be a real number such that $f(u) = 0$ (this is possible because f is surjective). Then, $P(u, u)$ yields $g(u) = 0$ and $P(u, x)$ implies

$$f(u - 3f(x)) = uf(x).$$

Hence, we find by surjectivity of f that $f(u - 3x) = ux$ for all real x. This means that

$$f(x) = cx + a, \quad \forall x \in \mathbb{R}.$$

Plugging this back in the original equation, we get $c = 1$ (using $g(1) = -8$) and $a = 3$. Hence, the solution is

$$f(x) = x + 3 \quad \text{and} \quad g(x) = -2x - 6, \quad \forall x \in \mathbb{R}.$$

One can simply check that this is a valid solution.

Problem 29. Find all functions $f : \mathbb{R}^+ \to \mathbb{R}^+$ such that

$$(x^2 + y^2)f(2017xf(y) + f(f(y))f(x)) = x^3 f(f(f(x))f(y))$$

for all $x, y \in \mathbb{R}^+$.

Solution (by pco). $f(x)$ is obviously injective. Setting $x = y = 2$ in the equation and using injectivity, we get $f(2) = 0$, which is impossible. So, no such function exists.

Problem 30. Determine all functions $f : \mathbb{R}^+ \to \mathbb{R}^+$ such that

$$f(x + f(x)f(y)) = f(x) + xf(y), \quad \forall x, y \in \mathbb{R}^+.$$

Solution (by pco). Let $P(x, y)$ be the assertion

$$f(x + f(x)f(y)) = f(x) + xf(y).$$

Note that choosing x great enough, we find that $f(\mathbb{R})$ is not upperbounded. We proceed in several steps.

1. **Claim.** If $f(x) < 1$, then $x < 1$.

   Proof: If $f(x) < 1$ for some $x > 0$, let $u = \frac{x}{1 - f(x)^2}$ so that $u - x = uf(x)^2$. Also, let $v = u + f(u)f(x)$ so that $P(u, x)$ implies $f(v) - f(u) = uf(x)$. So, we get

   $$u - x = uf(x)^2 = (f(v) - f(u))f(x),$$

   which means

   $$u + f(u)f(x) = x + f(x)f(v).$$

   Hence,

   $$f(u + f(u)f(x)) = f(x + f(x)f(v)),$$

and so

$$f(u) + uf(x) = f(x) + xf(v) = f(x) + x(f(u) + uf(x)).$$

Therefore,

$$f(u)(1 - x) = (1 + u(x - 1))f(x).$$

If $x \geq 1$, looking at the previous line, we get LHS $\leq 0 <$ RHS, which is impossible. So, $x < 1$ and we are done.

2. **Claim.** $f(x)$ is injective.

   Proof: Let $x > y > 0$ be real numbers such that $f(x) = f(y) = c > 0$. Define $u = \frac{x-y}{cf(r)}$ so that $x - y = ucf(r)$. Also, let $v = u + f(r)f(u)$ so that $f(v) = f(u) + uf(r)$. Then, we get $x - y = (f(v) - f(u))c$, which means

   $$x + f(x)f(u) = y + f(y)f(v).$$

   Thus,

   $$f(x + f(x)f(u)) = f(y + f(y)f(v)),$$

   which gives

   $$f(x) + xf(u) = f(y) + yf(v).$$

   Therefore, we find that

   $$xf(u) = yf(v) = y(f(u) + uf(r)),$$

   and so

   $$f(u) = \frac{yuf(r)}{x - y} = \frac{y}{c}.$$

   This means that

   $$f\left(\frac{x-y}{cf(r)}\right) = \frac{y}{c}, \quad \forall r > 0.$$

   Suppose that s is chosen so that $f(r) > f(s)$. Then, the latter result implies

   $$f\left(\frac{x-y}{cf(s)}\right) = f\left(\frac{x-y}{cf(r)}\right) = \frac{y}{c}.$$

   And so, applying the previous property,

   $$f\left(\frac{x-y}{y}\frac{f(r) - f(s)}{f(r)f(s)f(t)}\right) = \frac{x-y}{yf(r)}, \quad \forall r, s, t \text{ such that } f(r) > f(s).$$

Note that since $f(r)$ is not upperbounded, this implies that $\inf(f(\mathbb{R})) = 0$. Suppose now $f(r) > \frac{x-y}{y}$ so that RHS < 1. Using the fact that $f(x) < 1$ implies $x < 1$ which we proved in part 1, we get

$$f(t) > \frac{x-y}{y} \frac{f(r) - f(s)}{f(r)f(s)},$$

which is in contradiction with $\inf(f(\mathbb{R})) = 0$. So, $f(x)$ is injective.

3. **Claim.** $f(x) = x$ for all $x > 0$.

   Proof: Let $c = f(1)$ and consider a positive $x \neq 1$ (so that, since f is injective, $f(x) \neq c$). Then, subtracting $P(1, \frac{c}{f(x)})$ from $P(\frac{c}{f(x)}, x)$ and using injectivity, we get a new assertion which we call $R(x)$ as follows:

   $$f\left(\frac{c}{f(x)}\right) = \frac{1}{f(x)}, \qquad \forall x \neq 1.$$

   Then $R(\frac{c}{f(x)})$ implies $f(cf(x)) = f(x)$ for all $x \neq 1$. Now, injectivity implies $f(x) = \frac{x}{c}$ for all $x \neq 1$. If $c \neq 1$, setting $x = c^2$, we get $f(c^2) = c = f(1)$, impossible because of injectivity. Thus, $c = 1$ and $f(x) = x$ for all $x \neq 1$, still true when $x = 1$. It is easy to check that this function indeed fits the given equation.

4.2.4 Existence

Problem 31. Prove that there exists no function $f : \mathbb{R} \to \mathbb{R}$ satisfying

$$f(x + y) = e^x f(y) + e^y f(x) + xy, \qquad \forall x, y \in \mathbb{R}.$$

Solution (by pco). We have for all x, y, and z,

$$f(x + y + z) = e^x(e^y f(z) + e^z f(y) + yz) + e^{y+z} f(x) + x(y + z)$$
$$= e^{x+y} f(z) + e^{x+z} f(y) + e^{y+z} f(x) + xy + xz + e^x yz$$

Swapping x, y and subtracting, we get:

$$yz + e^y xz = xz + e^x yz, \qquad \forall x, y, z \in \mathbb{R},$$

which is clearly wrong.

Problem 32. Prove that there exist infinitely many functions f defined on $\mathbb{N}$ such that for all $n, k \in \mathbb{N}$, the following equation holds:

$$f(nf(k) + kf(n)) = f(n^2 + k^2)f(n + k - 1).$$

Solution (by pco). Choose for example

$$f(n) = a(1 + (-1)^n) + \frac{1 - (-1)^n}{2},$$

which is solution, whatever is $a \in \mathbb{N}$.

Problem 33. Does there exist a function f (defined on reals) which is continuous at the point $x = 0$ and $nf(nx) = f(x) + nx$, for a given integer $n \geq 2$ and all reals x?

Solution (by pco). Let $g(x) = xf(x)$. Then, g is continuous at 0 and has the property $g(nx) = g(x) + nx^2$. So,

$$g(x) = g\left(\frac{x}{n}\right) + x^2 \frac{1}{n}.$$

This gives us then

$$g(x) = g\left(\frac{x}{n^2}\right) + x^2 \left(\frac{1}{n} + \frac{1}{n^3}\right).$$

Similarly, one can easily show that

$$g(x) = g\left(\frac{x}{n^k}\right) + x^2 \sum_{i=1}^{k} \frac{1}{n^{2i-1}}.$$

Setting $k \to +\infty$ and using continuity at 0, we get $g(x) = g(0) + ax^2$, where

$$a = \sum_{i=1}^{+\infty} \frac{1}{n^{2i-1}},$$

which is never a solution. Thus, no such f exists.

Problem 35. Prove that there is no function $f : \mathbb{R}^+ \to \mathbb{R}$ such that for all positive x, y,

$$f(x + y) > y(f(x)^2).$$

Solution (by pco). Let $P(x, y)$ be the assertion $f(x + y) > yf(x)^2$. Let $x > 0$. Then

$$P\left(\frac{x}{2}, \frac{x}{2}\right) \implies f(x) > 0, \quad \forall x > 0.$$

Let then $a > 0$ and $x \in [0, a]$. We have

$$P(x, 2a - x) \implies f(2a) > (2a - x)f(x)^2 \geq af(x)^2$$

and so

$$f(x)^2 < \frac{f(2a)}{a}.$$

Hence, $f(x)$ is upper bounded over any interval $(0, a]$. Let then $f(1) = u > 0$ and define the sequence $\{x_n\}$ as $x_0 = 1$ and

$$x_{n+1} = x_n + \frac{2}{f(x_n)}, \quad \forall n \geq 0.$$

We get

$$P\left(x_n, \frac{2}{f(x_n)}\right) \implies f(x_{n+1}) > 2f(x_n)$$

and so $f(x_n) > 2^n u$ for all $n > 0$. Therefore,

$$x_1 = 1 + \frac{2}{u}$$

and

$$x_{n+1} < x_n + \frac{1}{2^{n-1}u}$$

for all $n > 0$. So,

$$x_n < 1 + \frac{1}{u}\left(2 + 1 + \frac{1}{2} + \frac{1}{4} + \cdots + \frac{1}{2^{n-1}}\right)$$
$$< 1 + \frac{4}{u}.$$

But $f(x_n) > 2^n u$ and $x_n < 1 + \frac{4}{u}$ shows that $f(x)$ is not upper bounded over $(0, 1 + \frac{4}{u}]$, and so contradiction with the first sentence of this proof. So, no such function exists.

4.2.5   Trigonometric and Periodic Functions

Problem 36. Let f be a function from the set of real numbers $\mathbb{R}$ into itself such for all $x \in \mathbb{R}$, we have $|f(x)| \leq 1$ and

$$f\left(x + \frac{13}{42}\right) + f(x) = f\left(x + \frac{1}{6}\right) + f\left(x + \frac{1}{7}\right).$$

Prove that f is a periodic function (that is, there exists a non-zero real number c such $f(x + c) = f(x)$ for all $x \in \mathbb{R}$).

Solution (by pco). Let $a = 1/6$ and $b = 1/7$. The equation is

$$f(x + a + b) + f(x) = f(x + a) + f(x + b).$$

Then

$$f(x + 2a + b) + f(x + a) = f(x + 2a) + f(x + a + b)$$
$$= f(x + 2a) + f(x + a) + f(x + b) - f(x),$$

and so

$$f(x + 2a + b) + f(x) = f(x + 2a) + f(x + b).$$

We can easily prove by induction that

$$f(x + na + b) + f(x) = f(x + na) + f(x + b), \quad \forall n \in \mathbb{N}.$$

Using the same method, one can find

$$f(x + na + mb) + f(x) = f(x + na) + f(x + mb), \quad \forall m, n \in \mathbb{N}.$$

Setting $n = 6$ and $m = 7$, this becomes

$$f(x + 2) = 2f(x + 1) - f(x).$$

If $f(x + 1) \neq f(x)$ this implies that $f(x + n)$ is unbounded, in contradiction with $f(x) \in [-1; +1], \forall x$. Hence,

$$f(x + 1) = f(x), \quad \forall x \in \mathbb{R},$$

and the proof is complete.

Problem 38. Does there exist a surjective and periodic function f on reals so that $f(x + 1) - f(x) = c$ for all $x \in \mathbb{R}$, where c is a fixed real number?

Solution (by pco). Here is a proof of existence using continuum hypothesis. Let

$$A = \{m + n\pi \quad \forall m, n \in \mathbb{Z}\}.$$

Then, A is an additive subgroup and so we can define an equivalence relation in A:

$$x \sim y \iff (x - y) \in A.$$

Let $r : \mathbb{R} \to \mathbb{R}$ be any function which associates to any real x a representative (unique per class) of its equivalence class. Let $B = r(\mathbb{R})$. Since any real x may be written in a unique manner as

$$x = r(x) + m(x) + n(x)\pi,$$

where $m(x)n(x) \in \mathbb{Z}$, we can conclude that B is uncountable, else $\{r(x) + m(x) + n(x)\pi\}$ would be countable (as it is $\sim \mathbb{N}^3$).

Therefore, by continuum hypothesis, there exists a bijection g from B to $\mathbb{R}$. Let us then define $f(x) = g(r(x)) + cm(x)$:

1. $m(x+1) = m(x) + 1$ and $r(x+1) = r(x)$, and so $f(x+1) = f(x) + c$.

2. $m(x+\pi) = m(x)$ and $r(x+\pi) = r(x)$, and so $f(x+\pi) = f(x)$ periodic.

3. $f(r(x)) = g(r(x))$ and $g(B) = \mathbb{R}$, and so $f(x)$ is surjective

The proof is complete.

Problem 39. Given real number $a \notin \{-1, 0, 1\}$, find all functions $f : \mathbb{R} \to \mathbb{R}$ such that
$$f(f(x) + ay) = (a^2 + a)x + f(f(y) - x)$$
for all reals x and y.

Solution (by pco). Let $P(x, y)$ be the given assertion and let $b = f(0)$. Since $a \neq 0$, $P(x, -\frac{f(x)}{a})$ implies
$$f(0) - (a^2 + a)x = f\left(f\left(-\frac{f(x)}{a}\right) - x\right).$$

Since $a^2 + a \neq 0$, LHS can take any value we want and so $f(x)$ is surjective. If $f(u) = f(v)$, subtracting $P(x, u)$ from $P(x, v)$ implies
$$f(f(x) + au) = f(f(x) + av)$$
and so, since f is surjective,
$$f(x + au) = f(x + av),$$
and so $f(x)$ is periodic with period $T = a(u - v)$. Subtracting then $P(x, y)$ from $P(x + T, y)$, we get $T = 0$ (since $a^2 + a \neq 0$) and so $f(x)$ is injective. Then $P(0, x)$ gives $f(f(x)) = f(ax + b)$ and so, since f is injective,
$$f(x) = ax + b, \quad \forall x \in \mathbb{R}$$
which indeed is a solution, whatever is $b \in \mathbb{R}$.

4.2.6 Functions Combined with Polynomials

Problem 41. Let $g(x)$ be a polynomial with real coefficients. Find all functions $f : \mathbb{R} \to \mathbb{R}$ that satisfy

$$\lfloor f(xg(x^2)) \rfloor = \lfloor f(g(x))^2 \rfloor + 1397$$

for all $x \in \mathbb{R}$.

Solution (by pco). Let $a = f(g(1))$. Setting $x = 1$ in the equation, we get

$$\lfloor a \rfloor = \lfloor a^2 \rfloor + 1397.$$

So,

$$(a^2 - 1) + 1397 < \text{RHS} = \text{LHS} \leq a.$$

This means $a^2 - a + 1396 < 0$, which is impossible. Hence, no solutions.

Problem 43. Find all functions $f : \mathbb{R} \to \mathbb{R}$ which satisfy

(i) $f(x + y) = f(x) + f(y)$ for all real x, y, and

(ii) $f(p(x)) = p(f(x))$ for some polynomial $p(x)$ of degree ≥ 2.

Solution (by pco). Let

$$p(x + y) = \sum a_{ij} x^i y^j.$$

We break the proof into three parts.

(1) **Claim.** There exists an even positive i such that $a_{ij} \neq 0$.
    Proof: if $a_{ij} = 0$ for all even positive i, then $p(x + y) = h(x, y) + q(y)$ with $h(-x, y) = -h(x, y)$. So,

$$p(x + y) + p(-x + y) = 2q(y),$$

and hence,

$$p(x) + p(-x) = 2q(0) \quad \text{and} \quad p(-x + y) = 2q(0) - p(x - y).$$

Then $p(x + y) + p(-x + y) = 2q(y)$ becomes $p(x + y) - p(x - y) = 2q(y) - 2q(0)$, and so for example $p(x + 1) - p(x)$ is a constant, which implies $\deg p \leq 1$, a contradiction.

(2) **Claim.** $f(x)$ is linear.
 Proof: Let $c = f(1)$ and $k \in \mathbb{Q}$. Then,

$$f(p(x+k)) = \sum a_{ij} f(x^i) k^j, \text{ and}$$
$$p(f(x+k)) = \sum a_{ij} f(x)^i c^j k^j.$$

Subtracting, we get

$$\sum a_{ij} (f(x^i) - f(x)^i c^j) k = 0.$$

Considering this as a polynomial in k with infinitely many roots (all rational numbers), we conclude that this is the all-zero polynomial. Therefore,

$$a_{ij}(f(x^i) - f(x)^i c^j) = 0, \quad \forall i, j.$$

Choosing one even positive i and a j such that $a_{ij} \neq 0$ (using part (1) above), we get $f(x^i) = f(x)^i c^j$ and so $f(x)$ has a constant sign over $\mathbb{R}^+$. So, $f(x)$ is either overbounded or lowerbounded over a non-empty open interval, and so is linear.

(3) So $f(x) = cx$ and $cp(x) = p(cx)$ for all $x \in \mathbb{R}$. Looking at highest degree summand in this last equality, we get $c \in \{-1, 0, 1\}$.

- $c = 0$ implies the solution

$$f(x) = 0, \quad \forall x \in \mathbb{R},$$

  which indeed is a solution if $p(0) = 0$.
- $c = 1$ implies the solution

$$f(x) = x, \quad \forall x \in \mathbb{R},$$

  which indeed is a solution.
- $c = -1$ implies the solution

$$f(x) = -x, \quad \forall x \in \mathbb{R},$$

  which indeed is a solution if $p(x)$ is an odd polynomial.

4.2.7 Functions on $\mathbb{R}^+$

Problem 45. For all functions $f, g : \mathbb{R}^+ \to \mathbb{R}^+$ that satisfy $f(1) = g(1)$ and for all positive x and y,

$$f(g(x) + y) = f(x) + g(y), \text{ and}$$
$$g(f(x) + y) = g(x) + f(y).$$

Prove that $f(x) = g(x)$ for all $x \in \mathbb{R}^+$.

Solution (by pco). Let $P(x, y)$ be the assertion $f(g(x) + y) = f(x) + g(y)$ and $Q(x; y)$ be the assertion $g(f(x) + y) = g(x) + f(y)$.

1. **Claim.** $f(x) \geq x$ and $g(x) \geq x$ for all $x > 0$. *Proof:* If $f(x) < x$ for some x, then $Q(x, x - f(x))$ gives a contradiction. So $f(x) \geq x$ for any $x > 0$. If $g(x) < x$ for some x, then $P(x, x - g(x))$ implies a contradiction. So, $g(x) \geq x$ for any $x > 0$.

2. **Claim.** If $f(x+a) = f(x)+b$ for all $x > 0$, then $a = b$. *Proof:* Suppose that there exists $a > 0$ and b such that $f(x+a) = f(x)+b$ holds for all $x > 0$. Subtracting $P(y, x)$ from $P(y, x+a)$, we get $g(x+a) = g(x)+b$ for all $x > 0$. Subtracting $P(1, x - g(1))$ from $P(1 + a, x - g(1))$, we get $f(x + b) = f(x) + b = f(x + a)$ for all $x > 0$ such that $x > g(1)$. Let $T = |a - b|$, then this implies $f(x + T) = f(x)$ for great enough x. But this implies $f(x) = f(x + nT) \geq x + nT$, impossible if $T \neq 0$ (set $n \to +\infty$ to see this).

3. **Claim.** $g(x) - f(x)$ is constant. *Proof:* Adding $Q(y, x)$ and $P(z, f(y) + x)$, we get
$$f(x + f(y) + g(z)) = f(x) + g(y) + f(z)$$
for all $x, y, z \in \mathbb{R}^+$. Therefore, using the second claim,
$$f(y) + g(z) = g(y) + f(z),$$
which is equivalent to $g(y) - f(y) = g(z) - f(z)$. The proof is complete.

Now, since $f(1) = g(1)$, by the last claim, we get the required conclusion.

Problem 47. Find all functions $f : \mathbb{R}^+ \to \mathbb{R}^+$ that satisfy
$$f(f(x) + 2y) = f(2x + y) + 2y$$
for all positive reals x and y.

Solution (by pco). Let $P(x,y)$ be the assertion

$$f(f(x) + 2y) = f(2x + y) + 2y.$$

Suppose $f(x+a) = f(x) + b$ for all $x > c$ for some $a, b \in \mathbb{R}$ and $c \in \mathbb{R}^+$. Choosing $y > c$ and subtracting $P(x,y)$ from $P(x, y+a)$, we get $b = 2a$.
Subtracting $P(z, f(y)/2 + x)$ from $P(y, f(z)/2 + x)$, we get

$$f(x + 2z + \frac{f(y)}{2}) = f(x + 2y + \frac{f(z)}{2}) + f(z) - f(y).$$

This is $f(x + u) = f(x + v) + w$ with

$$u = 2z + \frac{f(y)}{2}, \quad v = 2y + \frac{f(z)}{2}, \quad \text{and} \quad w = f(z) - f(y),$$

which is $f(x + u - v) = f(x) + w$ for all $x > v$, and therefore $w = 2(u - v)$. This gives

$$f(z) - f(y) = 2 \left(\left(2z + \frac{f(y)}{2} \right) - \left(2y + \frac{f(z)}{2} \right) \right).$$

Hene, $f(z) - 2z = f(y) - 2y$ and so $f(x) = 2x + a$ for some $a \in \mathbb{R}$. Plugging this back in original equation, we get $a = 0$ and so $f(x) = 2x$ for all $x > 0$.

Problem 50. Find all functions $f : \mathbb{R}^+ \to \mathbb{R}^+$ such that for all $x, y \in \mathbb{R}^+$,

$$f(3f(xy)^2 + (xy)^2) = (xf(y) + yf(x))^2.$$

Solution (by pco). Let $P(x,y)$ be the given assertion. Let $c = f(1)$. Subtracting $P(xy, 1)$ from $P(x, y)$ and remembering $f(x) > 0$ for all x, we get

$$xf(y) + yf(x) = cxy + f(xy).$$

Setting there

$$h(x) = e^{-x} f(e^x) - c,$$

where $h : \mathbb{R} \to (-c, +\infty)$ is a function, we get

$$h(x + y) = h(x) + h(y)$$

and so $h \equiv 0$ (lowerbounded over $\mathbb{R}$). So $f(x) = cx$ for all $x > 0$ and plugging this back in the original equation, we get $c \in \{\frac{1}{3}, 1\}$ and so the solutions are

- $f(x) = \frac{x}{3}, \quad \forall x > 0.$

- $f(x) = x, \quad \forall x > 0.$

Problem 51. Find all functions $f : \mathbb{R}^+ \to \mathbb{R}^+$ such that

$$f(x + f(y)) = f(x) - x + f(x + y)$$

for all positive real numbers x, y.

Solution (by pco). Let $P(x, y)$ be the given assertion. Notice that $P(x + f(z), y)$ gives

$$f(x + f(y) + f(z)) = f(x + f(z)) - x - f(z) + f(x + y + f(z)).$$

Also,

$$P(x, z) \implies f(x + f(z)) = f(x) - x + f(x + z)$$
$$P(x + y, z) \implies f(x + y + f(z)) = f(x + y) - x - y + f(x + y + z)$$

Adding, we get

$$f(x + f(y) + f(z)) = f(x) + f(x + z) + f(x + y) \tag{4.1}$$
$$- 3x - y - f(z) + f(x + y + z). \tag{4.2}$$

Swapping y and z in the above equation gives

$$f(x + f(y) + f(z)) = f(x) + f(x + y) + f(x + z) \tag{4.3}$$
$$- 3x - z - f(y) + f(x + y + z). \tag{4.4}$$

Subtracting (4.2) from (4.4), we find $f(z) - z = f(y) - y$. Thus,

$$f(x) = x + a, \quad \forall x > 0,$$

which indeed is a solution, whatever is $a \geq 0$.

Problem 52. Find all functions $f \colon \mathbb{R}^+ \to \mathbb{R}^+$ satisfying

$$f\left(f(xy) - xy\right) + xf(y) + yf(x) = f(xy) + f(x)f(y), \quad \forall x, y \in \mathbb{R}^+.$$

Solution (by pco). Let $P(x, y)$ be the given assertion. Note that, in order for LHS to be defined, we must have $f(x) > x$ for all x in the domain. Define $c = \ln(f(1) - 1)$. Subtracting $P(xy, 1)$ from $P(x, y)$, we get

$$e^c(f(xy) - xy) = (f(x) - x)(f(y) - y).$$

So, $e^{-c}(f(x) - x)$ is positive multiplicative over $\mathbb{R}^+$. Hence,

$$f(x) - x = e^{c + g(\ln x)},$$

where $g(x)$ is some additive function over $\mathbb{R}$. Plugging this in the original equation, we get $g(c) = c$ and $g(g(x)) = g(x)$.

Thus, a general solution is: let A, B be any two supplementary sub-vectorspaces of the $\mathbb{Q}$-vectorspace $\mathbb{R}$. Also, let $a : \mathbb{R} \to A$ and $b : \mathbb{R} \to B$ be the two projections of a real x in (A, B) and consider any $c \in A$. Then,

$$f(x) = x + e^{c + a(\ln x)}, \quad \forall x > 0.$$

Problem 53. Prove that there are no functions $f : \mathbb{R}^+ \to \mathbb{R}^+$ such that

$$(x + y)f(f(x)y) = x^2 f(f(x) + f(y)), \quad \forall x, y \in \mathbb{R}^+.$$

Solution (by pco). Let $P(x, y)$ be the given assertion. It is easy to see that $f(x)$ is injective. Then, $P(3/2, 3/4)$ implies

$$f\left(\frac{3}{4}\right) + \frac{1}{4}f\left(\frac{3}{2}\right) = 0,$$

which is impossible since $f(x) > 0$. So, no such function exists.

Problem 54. Find all functions $f : \mathbb{R}^+ \to \mathbb{R}$ that satisfy

$$f(x - y)^2 = f(x)^2 - 2f(xy) + f(y)^2$$

for all real x and y with $x > y > 0$.

Solution (by pco). Let $P(x, y)$ be the assertion

$$f(x - y)^2 = f(x)^2 - 2f(xy) + f(y)^2.$$

Adding $P(x, y)$ to $P(x, x - y)$, we get

$$f(x)^2 = f(x^2 - xy) + f(xy), \quad \forall x > y > 0.$$

Changing $y \mapsto y/x$, this becomes

$$f(x)^2 = f(x^2 - y) + f(y), \quad \forall x > 0 \text{ and } \forall y \in (0, x^2). \tag{4.5}$$

Then,

$$P\left(x, \frac{x}{2}\right) \implies f(x)^2 = 2f\left(\frac{x^2}{2}\right),$$

which implies $f(x) \geq 0$ for all $x > 0$. Plugging this in (4.5), we get

$$2f\left(\frac{x^2}{2}\right) = f(x^2 - y) + f(y), \quad \forall x > 0 \text{ and } y \in (0, x^2).$$

This means that

$$f(\frac{x+y}{2}) = \frac{f(x) + f(y)}{2}, \quad \forall x, y > 0.$$

Since $f(x) \geq 0$ for any positive x, this is classical Jensen's functional equation and the solution is $f(x) = ax + b$. Plugging this back in original equation, we get the solutions

- $f \equiv 0$.

- $f \equiv 2$.

- $f(x) = x$ for all $x > 0$.

Problem 55. Find all functions $f, g : \mathbb{R}^+ \to \mathbb{R}^+$ such that

$$f(x + f(y)) = \{y\} + g(x)$$

holds for all positive reals x and y. Here, $\{y\}$ is the fractional part of y. That is, $\{y\} = y - \lfloor y \rfloor$.

Solution (by pco). Let $P(x, y)$ be the assertion

$$f(x + f(y)) = \{y\} + g(x).$$

Define $a = f(1)$. Then, $P(x, 1)$ implies $g(x) = f(x+a)$ and so we define the new assertion $Q(x, y)$ as

$$f(x + f(y)) = \{y\} + f(x + a).$$

One can then easily prove by induction that

$$f(x + nf(y)) = n\{y\} + f(x + na)$$

holds for all positive integers n. This implies that $f(x)$ in not upperbounded and that we can find in $f(\mathbb{R})$ segments as large as we want. If $f(x)$ is periodic from a given point s with some period $T > 0$, then let $n > 2(f(2a) + 1)$ and $x = s$ so that $f(x + nf(y)) = n\{y\} + f(x + na)$ implies

$$f\left(s + nf\left(\frac{1}{2}\right)\right) > 1 + f(2a)$$

and therefore,

$$f(t + kT) > 1 + f(2a), \quad \forall k \in \mathbb{N},$$

for some $t = s + nf(1/2)$. Since we can find in $f(\mathbb{R})$ segments as large as we want, let $\Delta > t + T$ and U such that $[U, U + \Delta] \subset f(\mathbb{R})$. Then, $Q(a, x)$ yields

$$f(a + f(x)) = \{x\} + f(2a) \in [f(2a), f(2a) + 1).$$

Thus,

$$f(x) < 1 + f(2a), \quad \forall x \in [U + a, U + a + \Delta].$$

But this is in contradiction with $f(t + kT) > 1 + f(2a)$. Therefore, $f(x)$ can not be periodic from a given point and the equation $f(x + u) = f(x + v)$ (for all $x > 0$) would imply $u = v$. Now, for any $n \in \mathbb{N}$, $P(x, y + n)$ implies

$$f(x + f(y)) = f(x + f(y + n)),$$

and so $f(y + n) = f(y)$, which is impossible. Hence, no such functions f and g exist.

Problem 57. Find all functions $f : \mathbb{R}^+ \to \mathbb{R}^+$ satisfying the equation

$$f(x + f(xy)) = xf(1 + f(y))$$

for all positive x and y.

Solution (by Roman Buzuk from Belarus). Let $P(x, y)$ be the given assertion. Calculating $P(x, 1)$, we find $f(x + f(x)) = xf(1 + f(1))$. Set $C = f(1 + f(1))$. Then,

$$f(x + f(x)) = Cx, \quad \forall x \in \mathbb{R}^+.$$

Now, for any $t > 0$, $P(f(t) + t, 1)$ gives

$$f(t + f(t) + f(t + f(t))) = f(t + f(t) + Ct) = C(t + f(t)).$$

By $P((C+1)t, 1/(C+1))$, we get that

$$f((C+1)t + f(t)) = (C+1)tf\left(1 + f\left(\frac{1}{C+1}\right)\right) = C(t + f(t)).$$

It now makes sense to define D as

$$D = \frac{(C+1)f(1 + f(\frac{1}{C+1}))}{C} - 1,$$

so that $f(t) = Dt$ for all $t > 0$. We can easily check that this is indeed a solution:

$$xf(1 + f(y)) = Dx + D^2xy = f(x + Dxy) = f(x + f(xy)).$$

Hence, $f(x) = Dx$ for all $x \in \mathbb{R}^+$ is the only solution.

Problem 61. Find all functions $f : \mathbb{R}^+ \to \mathbb{R}^+$ such that for all $x, y \in \mathbb{R}^+$,

$$f(f(x) + x + y) = x\left(1 + xf\left(\frac{1}{x+y}\right)\right).$$

Solution (by pco). Let $P(x, y)$ be the assertion

$$f(f(x) + x + y) = x + x^2f\left(\frac{1}{x+y}\right).$$

Now, substituting $P(1, x + y - 1)$ implies

$$f(f(1) + x + y) = 1 + f\left(\frac{1}{x+y}\right), \quad \forall x + y > 1$$

Plugging this in $P(x, y)$, we get the new assertion $Q(x, y)$:

$$f(f(x) + y) = x - x^2 + x^2 f(y + f(1)), \quad \forall y > \max(x, 1).$$

Plug in $Q(x, y + f(z))$ to find

$$f(f(x)+f(z)+y) = x-x^2+x^2f(y+f(z)+f(1)), \forall y > \max(0, x-f(z), 1-f(z)).$$

Also, $Q(z, y + f(1))$ implies

$$f(f(z)+y+f(1)) = z-z^2+z^2f(y+2f(1)), \quad \forall y > \max(0, z-f(1), 1-f(1)).$$

Combining, we get

$$f(f(x) + f(z) + y) = x - x^2 + x^2(z - z^2 + z^2f(y + 2f(1))),$$
$$\forall y > \max(0, x - f(z), 1 - f(z), z - f(1), 1 - f(1)).$$

Swapping x, z and subtracting (for y great enough), this implies

$$x - x^2 + x^2(z - z^2) = z - z^2 + z^2(x - x^2), \quad \forall x, z \in \mathbb{R}^+,$$

which is wrong. So, there is no such function.

4.2.8   Sequences

Problem 63. Find an infinite family of solutions $f : \mathbb{R} \to \mathbb{R}$ for which $(f(1+2x))^2 = x - (f(1-x))^3$ holds for all $x \in \mathbb{R}$.

Solution (by pco). Writing $g(x) = f(x+1)$, the functional equation becomes

$$g(-2x)^2 = -x - g(x)^3.$$

Let $h : [2,8) \to \mathbb{R}^-$ be any function such that $h(x) \leq \sqrt[3]{-x}$ for all $x \in [2,8)$. Let then $a \in [2,8)$ and define the sequences $\{a_n\}$ and $\{b_n\}$ as

$$a_0 = h(a) \text{ and } a_{n+1} = \sqrt[3]{-\frac{a}{(-2)^{n+1}} - a_n^2} \text{ for all } n \geq 0$$

and

$$b_0 = h(a) \text{ and } b_{n+1} = -\sqrt{-(-2)^n a - b_n^3} \text{ for all } n \geq 0.$$

Claim. The sequence b_n is well-defined. That is, the quantity inside the square root is non-negative.

Proof: Clearly, b_0 is defined and is less than $\sqrt[3]{-a}$. So, $b_1 = -\sqrt{-a - b_0^3}$ is well-defined. Suppose then b_{2n-1} is well-defined and negative for some $n \in \mathbb{N}$. Then,

$$-(-2)^{2n-1}a > 0 \text{ and } - b_{2n-1}^3 > 0,$$

and so

$$b_{2n} = -\sqrt{-(-2)^{2n-1}a - b_{2n-1}^3}$$

is indeed well-defined. Note that the above line implies $-b_{2n} \geq \sqrt{2^{2n-1}a}$. Hence,

$$-b_{2n}^3 \geq 2^{\frac{6n-3}{2}} a^{\frac{3}{2}},$$

and it is easy to show that $a \geq 2$ implies

$$2^{\frac{6n-3}{2}} a^{\frac{3}{2}} \geq 2^{2n}a.$$

Therefore, $-(-2)^{2n}a - b_{2n}^3 \geq 0$ and this yields

$$b_{2n+1} = -\sqrt{-(-2)^{2n}a - b_{2n}^3}$$

is well-defined. This proves our claim that b_n is well defined for all $n \in \mathbb{Z}^{\geq 0}$.

From here, we easily get that defining

$$g\left(\frac{a}{(-2)^n}\right) = a_n \text{ and } g((-2)^n a) = b_n$$

gives consistent values for $g(x)$ for all $x = a(-2)^n$, where n is an integer. Applying this method for all $a \in [2, 8)$, gives full consistent values for $g(x)$ all over $\mathbb{R} \setminus \{0\}$. Choosing any $g(0) \in \{0, -1\}$ ends the full consistent definition of $g(x)$ all over $\mathbb{R}$.

Problem 65. Find all functions f defined om $\mathbb{R}^+$ such that $f(0) = 0$ and

$$f(x) = 1 + 7f\left(\left\lfloor \frac{x}{2} \right\rfloor\right) - 6f\left(\left\lfloor \frac{x}{4} \right\rfloor\right)$$

for all $x > 0$.

Solution (by pco). Setting $x = 1$, we get $f(1) = 1$. Setting $x = 2$, we get $f(2) = 8$. Let $a_n = f(2^n)$ and we get $a_0 = 1$, $a_1 = 8$ and

$$a_{n+2} = 1 + 7a_{n+1} - 6a_n.$$

This is easily solved as

$$a_n = \frac{6^{n+2} - 5n - 11}{25}.$$

From there, it is immediate to get $f(x) = 1$ for all $x \in (0, 2)$ and

$$f(x) = f(2^n) = \frac{6^{n+2} - 5n - 11}{25}, \quad \forall x \in [2^n, 2^{n+1}), n \in \mathbb{N}$$

So,

$$f(x) = \frac{6^{\max(0, \lfloor \log_2 x \rfloor) + 2} - 5\max(0, \lfloor \log_2 x \rfloor) - 11}{25}, \quad \forall x > 0.$$

Problem 66. Find all functions $f : \mathbb{R}^+ \to \mathbb{R}^+$ such that

$$f(2016 + xf(y)) = yf(x + y + 2016),$$

for all $x, y \in \mathbb{R}^+$.

Solution (by pco). Define $c = 2016$ for easier writing. Let $P(x, y)$ be the assertion $f(c + xf(y)) = yf(x + y + c)$. If $f(x) > 1$ for some $x > 0$, then

$$P\left(\frac{x}{f(x) - 1}, x\right) \implies x = 1.$$

So, $f(x) \leq 1$ for all $x \neq 1$. Therefore, $f(c + xf(y)) \leq 1$ and so

$$f(x + y + c) \leq \frac{1}{y}, \quad \forall x, y > 0.$$

The latter equation can be written as

$$f(x+c) \leq \frac{1}{y}, \quad \forall x > y > 0.$$

And so, setting $y \mapsto x^-$, we find that

$$f(x+c) \leq \frac{1}{x}, \quad \forall x > 0.$$

Let $a = f(1)$.

1. If $a \leq 1$, let us consider the sequence $\{u_n\}$ defined as $u_1 = x$ and for all $n \geq 1$,
$$u_{n+1} = \frac{u_n}{a} + 1.$$

This sequence is increasing with limit $+\infty$. Now,

$$P\left(\frac{u_n}{a}, 1\right) \implies f(u_n + c) = f(u_{n+1} + c),$$

and so

$$f(x+c) = f(u_n + c) \leq \frac{1}{u_n},$$

which means $f(x+c) = 0$, impossible.

2. If $a > 1$, consider $x > \frac{a}{a-1} > 1$. Define the sequence $\{u_n\}$ by $u_1 = x$ and for all $n \geq 1$,
$$u_{n+1} = a(u_n - 1).$$

The sequence is increasing with limit $+\infty$. Then, $P(u_n - 1, 1)$ yields $f(u_n + c) = f(u_{n+1} + c)$, and so

$$f(x+c) = f(u_n + c) \leq \frac{1}{u_n}.$$

This means that $f(x+c) = 0$, which is, again, impossible.

Thus, there are no solutions.

4.2.9   Inequalities

Problem 67. Find all functions $f : \mathbb{R}^+ \to \mathbb{R}^+$ such that for all $x, y \in \mathbb{R}^+$, the following conditions are satisfied:

(i) $f(x+y) \geq f(x) + y$, and

(ii) $f(f(x)) \le x$.

Solution (by pco). Notice that (i) implies $f(x)$ is strictly increasing and then (ii) implies $f(x) \le x$. By (i), we find that

$$f(x) \ge f(x - y) + y > y, \quad \forall y \in (0, x).$$

Setting there $y \mapsto x^-$, we get $f(x) \ge x$ for all $x > 0$. Therefore,

$$f(x) = x, \quad \forall x > 0,$$

which indeed is a solution.

Problem 68. Find all functions $f : \mathbb{R}^+ \to \mathbb{R}$ satisfying the inequality

$$f(x) - f(y) \ge \ln\left(\frac{x}{y}\right) + x - y$$

for all $x, y \in \mathbb{R}^+$.

Solution (by pco). The inequality is equivalent to

$$f(x) - \ln x - x \ge f(y) - \ln y - y, \quad \forall x, y \in \mathbb{R}^+.$$

Swapping x, y and comparing, we get

$$f(x) = x + \ln x + a, \quad \forall x > 0$$

for any choice of $a \in \mathbb{R}$. One can easily check that this is indeed a valid solution.

Problem 69. Find all real numbers a and functions $f : \mathbb{R} \to \mathbb{R}$ which satisfy the following conditions:

(i) $af(x) - x \le af(f(y)) - y$ holds for all real numbers x and y.

(ii) there is a real number x_0 is such that $f(x_0) = x_0$.

Solution (by pco). Let $P(x, y)$ be the assertion $af(x) - x \le af(f(y)) - y$. Then $P(f(x), x)$ implies $f(x) \ge x$ for all real x. If $a < 0$, then $f(f(y)) \ge f(y)$ yields $af(f(y)) \le af(y)$ and so

$$af(x) - x \le af(f(y)) - y \le af(y) - y.$$

This means $af(x) - x = c$, where c is a constant. But then $c = af(x) - x \leq ax - x$, which is impossible if $a < 0$. Therefore, $a \geq 0$ and so

$$(a-1)x \leq af(x) - x \leq af(f(y)) - y.$$

This in turn gives $a = 1$ and then $P(x, x_0)$ becomes

$$f(x) - x \leq f(f(x_0)) - x_0 = 0.$$

Hence,

$$f(x) = x, \quad \forall x \in \mathbb{R},$$

which is indeed a solution.

Problem 70. Find all functions $f : \mathbb{R}^+ \to \mathbb{R}$ satisfying

$$f(x) + f(y) \leq \frac{f(x+y)}{4}, \quad \text{and}$$
$$\frac{f(x)}{y} + \frac{f(y)}{x} \geq \left(\frac{1}{x} + \frac{1}{y}\right) \cdot \frac{f(x+y)}{8},$$

for all positive reals x, y.

Solution (by pco). Combine the two given inequalities and write them as assertion $P(x, y)$:

$$8\frac{xf(x) + yf(y)}{x+y} \geq f(x+y) \geq 4f(x) + 4f(y).$$

So,

$$8\frac{xf(x) + yf(y)}{x+y} \geq 4f(x) + 4f(y),$$

which can be represented as $(x - y)(f(x) - f(y)) \geq 0$. Therefore, $f(x) \geq f(y)$ for all $x > y$. Now, $P(x, x)$ implies that $f(2x) = 8f(x)$ and since $f(2x) \geq f(x)$, we get $f(x) \geq 0$ for all positive real x. So,

$$f(x + y) \geq 4f(x) + 4f(y) \geq 4f(x).$$

From here, induction gives $f(x+ny) \geq 4^n f(x)$ for all $n \in \mathbb{N}$. Setting $y = 1/n$ in the latter equation, we get $f(x+1) \geq 4^n f(x)$ for any $n \in \mathbb{N}$ and so, since $f(x) \geq 0$, $f \equiv 0$. One should check that this is indeed a solution.

Problem 73. Find all functions $f : \mathbb{R} \to \mathbb{R}$ such that for all real numbers a, b, and c:

(i) If $a + b + c \geq 0$ then $f(a^3) + f(b^3) + f(c^3) \geq 3f(abc)$.

(ii) If $a + b + c \leq 0$ then $f(a^3) + f(b^3) + f(c^3) \leq 3f(abc)$.

Solution (by Sutanay Bhattacharya). We claim that all solutions are of the form $f(x) \equiv cx + d$ for some $c \geq 0$. It's easy to check all such functions work, because of the identity

$$a^3 + b^3 + c^3 - 3abc = \tfrac{1}{2}(a + b + c)((a - b)^2 + (b - c)^2 + (c - a)^2).$$

If f is a function satisfying the conditions, then so is $f + k$ for any constant k, so we can assume, WLOG, that $f(0) = 0$. Note that the given statements imply the following:

For reals a, b, c with $a + b + c = 0$, we have $f(a^3) + f(b^3) + f(c^3) = 3f(abc)$.

Call this statement $P(a, b, c)$. Now $P(a^{\frac{1}{3}}, -a^{\frac{1}{3}}, 0)$ gives $f(a) + f(-a) = 0$, so f is odd. Now for $a > 0$, we have $a^{\frac{1}{3}} + 0 + 0 \geq 0$, so condition ($i$) gives $f(a) \geq 0$. Because of oddness, we have $f(a) \leq 0$ for $a < 0$. So f takes non-negative values at non-negative inputs and non-positive values for non-positive inputs.

Now consider that statement $P(a, b, -(a + b))$. Because f is odd, this translates into

$$f(a^3) + f(b^3) + 3f(ab(a + b)) = f((a + b)^3).$$

Using this equation multiple times, we obtain

$$\begin{aligned}
f((a + b + c)^3) &= f((a + b)^3) + f(c^3) + 3f((a + b)c(a + b + c)) \\
&= f(a^3) + f(b^3) + 3f(ab(a + b)) + f(c^3) \\
&\quad + 3f((a + b)c(a + b + c))
\end{aligned}$$

Similarly, switching the roles of b and c we get,

$$f((a+b+c)^3) = f(a^3) + f(b^3) + f(c^3) + 3f(ac(a+c)) + 3f((b(a+c)(a+b+c)).$$

Comparing these two expressions for $f((a + b + c)^3)$, we obtain

$$f(c(a + b)(a + b + c)) + f(ab(a + b)) = f(b(a + c)(a + b + c)) + f(ac(a + c)). \tag{4.6}$$

Now choose arbitrary positive reals $x \leq y$ and consider the following system of equations

$$a^2 c - abc = a^2 b + ab^2 \tag{4.7}$$

$$a^2 b + ab^2 = x \tag{4.8}$$

$$a^2 c + ac^2 = y \tag{4.9}$$

We claim that this has a solution in reals a, b, c. Indeed, set $b = qa, c = ra$, and (4.7) becomes

$$r - qr = q + q^2 \implies r = \frac{q^2 + q}{1 - q}.$$

Also, dividing (4.8) by (4.9), we get

$$\frac{x}{y} = \frac{q(q+1)}{r(r+1)} = \frac{q(q+1)}{\frac{q(q+1)}{1-q} \cdot \frac{q^2+1}{1-q}} = \frac{(q-1)^2}{1 + q^2}.$$

The function $h(q) = \frac{(q-1)^2}{1+q^2}$ is continuous on $[0, 1]$ and $h(0) = 1, h(1) = 0$. Since $\frac{x}{y} \in (0, 1]$, there is a $q \in [0, 1)$ so that $h(q) = \frac{x}{y}$. Choose this q, and the corresponding $r = \frac{q(q+1)}{1-q}$. Then scale both q and r by a to get b, c so that (4.8) holds; then (4.9) and (4.7) would hold automatically. Thus a, b, c exist; clearly $a \neq 0$.

Now that we've chosen suitable a, b, c, note that

$$a^2 c - abc = a^2 b + ab^2 \implies b(a + b + c) = ac$$
$$\implies b(a + c)(a + b + c) = ac(a + c) = y,$$

and

$$ab(a + b) = x,$$

so

$$c(a + b)(a + b + c) = (b(a + c)(a + b + c) + ac(a + c)) - ab(a + b)$$
$$= 2y - x.$$

Using these in (4.6) gives

$$f(2y - x) + f(x) = 2f(y) \; \forall 0 < x \leq y.$$

Setting $z = 2y - x \iff y = \frac{x+z}{2}$, this becomes

$$f(x) + f(z) = 2f\left(\frac{x + z}{2}\right) \; \forall 0 < x \leq z.$$

So f satisfies Jensen's functional equation over positives, and it's bounded on $[0, \infty)$, so $f(x) = cx + d$ for some $c \geq 0$, as claimed.

4.2.10   Miscellaneous

Innovative Problems

Problem 75. Find all function $f : \mathbb{R} \to \mathbb{R}$ so that

$$f(zf(x)f(y)) + f(f(z)(f(x) + f(y))) = f(xyz + xz + yz), \quad \forall x, y, z \in \mathbb{R}.$$

Solution (by pco). $f(x) = 0, \forall x$ is the only constant solution. So let us from now look only for non-constant solutions. Let $P(x, y, z)$ be the assertion

$$f(zf(x)f(y)) + f(f(z)(f(x) + f(y))) = f(xyz + xz + yz).$$

1. **Claim.** $f(x) = 0 \iff x = 0$.
   Proof: Let $a = f(0)$. Then, $P(0, 0, 0)$ implies $f(2a^2) = 0$ and then $P(2a^2, 2a^2, 0)$ yields $2a = a$. Therefore, $a = 0$. If $f(u) = 0$ for some $u \neq 0$, then $P(x, 0, u)$ gives $f(ux) = 0$, impossible since $f(x)$ is assumed to be a non-constant function.

2. **Claim.** The only injective solutions are $f(x) = x$ and $f(x) = -x$.
   Proof: $P(x, 0, 1)$ implies $f(f(1)f(x)) = f(x)$ and so, since f is injective, $f(x) = f(1)x$. Plugging this in $P(x, y, z)$, we get $f(1) \in \{-1, +1\}$ and the desired result follows.

3. **Claim.** There are no non-constant non-injective solutions.
   Proof: By the first part, $f(a) = f(b) = 0$ implies $a = b = 0$. If $f(a) = f(b) \neq 0$ for some $a \neq b$, then, subtracting $P(x, 0, a)$ from $P(x, 0, b)$, we get $f(ax) = f(bx)$ for all real x and so $f(ux) = f(x)$ holds for all x and some real $u = a/b \notin \{0, 1\}$. Comparing then $P(x, y, z)$ with $P(ux, y, z)$ where $x, y, z \in \mathbb{R}$, we observe that

$$f(uxyz + uxz + yz) = f(xyz + xz + yz).$$

Now, choosing $s \neq t$, it is easy to find x, y, z such that

$$xyz + xz + yz = s \text{ and } uxyz + uxz + yz = t.$$

Therefore, $f(s) = f(t)$ for all $s \neq t$, which is impossible since $f(x)$ is non-constant.

Problem 78. Determine all functions $f : \mathbb{R} \to \mathbb{R}$ such that:

$$f(\max\{x, y\} + \min\{f(x), f(y)\}) = x + y$$

for all real $x, y \in \mathbb{R}$

Solution (by pco). Let $P(x, y)$ be the assertion

$$f(\max(x, y) + \min(f(x), f(y))) = x + y.$$

Let $a = f(0)$. Then,

$$P(x, x) \implies f(x + f(x)) = 2x.$$

Suppose that x and y are reals such that $x > y$. If $f(x) \leq f(y)$, then

$$P(x, y) \implies f(x + f(x)) = x + y = 2x$$

and so $x = y$, impossible. Therefore, $x > y$ implies $f(x) > f(y)$ and

$$P(x, y) \implies f(x + f(y)) = x + y, \quad \forall x > y \qquad (4.10)$$

Hence, $f(x) = x + y - f(y)$ holds $\forall x > f(y)$. Setting there $y = 0$, we get

$$f(x) = x - a, \quad \forall x > a. \qquad (4.11)$$

Let then $y \in \mathbb{R}$ and $x > \max(y, a - f(y))$. Then, $x > y$ implies $f(x + f(y)) = x + y$ by (4.10) and $x + f(y) > a$ implies $f(x + f(y)) = x + f(y) - a$ by (4.11). Therefore,

$$f(y) = y + a, \quad \forall y \in \mathbb{R}.$$

Plugging this back in original equation, we get $a = 0$ and so

$$f(x) = x, \quad \forall x \in \mathbb{R}.$$

Problem 79. Find all real numbers c for which there exists a function $f : \mathbb{R} \to \mathbb{R}$ such that for all $x, y \in \mathbb{R}$,

$$f(f(x) + f(y)) + cxy = f(x + y).$$

Solution (by pco). Let $P(x, y)$ be the given assertion. Let $A = f(\mathbb{R})$ and $a = f(0)$. If $c = 0$, then we can easily choose $f(x) = x$ for all x.

1. If $c > 0$, then

$$P(x, -x) \implies f(f(x) + f(-x)) = cx^2 + a$$

and so $[a, +\infty) \subseteq A$. Also,

$$P(x, 0) \implies f(f(x) + a) = f(x)$$

and so $f(x) = x - a$ for all $x \geq 2a$. Let then x and y be reals such that $x, y \geq 2a$ and $x + y \geq \max(2a, 4a)$. Then, $P(x, y)$ becomes

$$x + y - 3a + cxy = x + y - a,$$

which is, obviously, impossible.

2. If $c < 0$, then

$$P(x, -x) \implies f(f(x) + f(-x)) = cx^2 + a$$

and so $(-\infty, a] \subseteq A$. Furthermore,

$$P(x, 0) \implies f(f(x) + a) = f(x)$$

and so $f(x) = x - a$ for any $x \leq 2a$. Take $x, y \leq 2a$ and $x + y \leq \min(2a, 4a)$. Then, $P(x, y)$ becomes

$$x + y - 3a + cxy = x + y - a,$$

which is, again, impossible.

Hence, the answer is $c = 0$.

Problem 80. Find all functions $f : \mathbb{R} \to \mathbb{R}$ that satisfy the following conditions:

a. $x + f(y + f(x)) = y + f(x + f(y)), \quad \forall x, y \in \mathbb{R}.$

b. The set

$$I = \left\{ \frac{f(x) - f(y)}{x - y} \mid x, y \in \mathbb{R}, x \neq y \right\}$$

is an interval. That is, for any $a, b \in I$ such that $a < b$, we have $[a, b] \subseteq I$.

Solution (by pco). Let $P(x, y)$ be the assertion

$$x + f(y + f(x)) = y + f(x + f(y)).$$

If $1 \in I$, then there exists $x \neq y$ such that $f(x) - f(y) = x - y$, and so $y + f(x) = x + f(y)$. Then, $P(x, y)$ implies $x = y$, which is a contradiction. So, $1 \notin I$. If $t \neq 1 \in I$, then let $x \neq y$ be real numbers such that

$$\frac{f(x) - f(y)}{x - y} = t.$$

Then, we have $x + f(y) \neq y + f(x)$ and

$$A = \frac{f(x + f(y)) - f(y + f(x))}{(x + f(y)) - (y + f(x))} = \frac{x - y}{(x - y) - (f(x) - f(y))} = \frac{1}{1 - t}.$$

Therefore, $t \in I$ implies $\frac{1}{1-t} \in I$ which is impossible because:

- If $t > 1$, then $\frac{1}{1-t} < 0$ and we can not have both in I (else $1 \in I$).

- If $t < 1$, then we need $1/(1 - t) < 1$, which means $t < 0$. But then $1/(1 - t) > 0$ and replacing t by $1/(1 - t)$ gives a contradiction.

Therefore, no such I exists and there are no functions f which satisfy the given conditions.

Problem 81. Let $f, g : \mathbb{R} \to \mathbb{R}$ be two quadratics such that for any real number r, if $f(r)$ is an integer, then $g(r)$ is also an integer. Prove that there are two integers m and n such that

$$g(x) = mf(x) + n, \quad \forall x \in \mathbb{R}.$$

Solution (by Catalin Dumitru). We will prove that f is monotonic, hence it will be continuous. Suppose that it is not. Then there are $x < y < z$ such that, WLOG, $f(x) < f(y)$ and $f(y) > f(z)$. Then, for any $\lambda \in I = (f(x), f(y)) \cap (f(z), f(y))$ there are $c_\lambda \in (x, y)$ and $d_\lambda \in (y, z)$ such that

$$f(c_\lambda) = f(d_\lambda) = \lambda.$$

Since f is injective on the irrationals, at least one of these two numbers will be rational, and let u_λ be the one. Now define

$$g : I \to \mathbb{Q}, \ g(\lambda) = u_\lambda.$$

We will prove that g is injective. Indeed, let $a, b \in I$ such that $g(a) = g(b)$. Then,

$$u_a = u_b \implies f(u_a) = f(u_b) \implies a = b.$$

Hence, there is an injection from I to $\mathbb{Q}$. Since $\mathbb{Q}$ is countable, there is also an injection from $\mathbb{Q}$ to $\mathbb{N}$, and thus there is an injection from I to $\mathbb{N}$. But this means that I, a non-empty interval, is countable, which is a contradiction. In conclusion, f is monotonic and so it is continuous.

Problem 82. Find all functions $f : \mathbb{R} \to \mathbb{R}$ such that

$$f(x - f(y)) = f(x + y) + f(f(y) + y)$$

for all real numbers x, y.

Solution (by pco). Let $P(x, y)$ be the assertion

$$f(x - f(y)) = f(x + y) + f(f(y) + y).$$

Define $a = f(0)$. Notice that

$$P(2a, 0) \implies f(2a) = 0,$$
$$P(0, 2a) \implies a = 0,$$
$$P(f(x), x) \implies f(x + f(x)) = 0, \quad \forall x \in \mathbb{R}.$$

Then $P(x + f(y), y)$ gives

$$f(x + (f(y) + y)) = f(x), \quad \forall x, y \in \mathbb{R}.$$

Hence, the general solutions have the form following form: let $A \subseteq \mathbb{R}$ be any additive subgroup of $\mathbb{R}$. Let $\sim$ be the equivalence relation over $\mathbb{R}$ defined as

$$x \sim y \iff x - y \in A.$$

Let $r : \mathbb{R} \to \mathbb{R}$ be any choice of function associating to a real x a representative (unique per class) of its equivalence class. Let $g : \mathbb{R} \to A$ be any function such that $g(r(0)) = r(0)$. Then, $f(x) = g(r(x)) - r(x)$.

Some examples:

- If $A = \mathbb{R}$, we get $f \equiv 0$.

- If $A = \{0\}$, we get $f(x) = -x$ for all real x.

- If $A = \mathbb{Z}$, $r(x) = \{x\}$, and $g(x) = \lfloor 2017 \sin(2\pi x) \rfloor$, we get

$$f(x) = \lfloor 2017 \sin(2\pi x) \rfloor - \{x\}.$$

Problem 83. Find all functions $f : \mathbb{R} \to \mathbb{R}$ satisfying

$$f(x + f(y)) = f(y^2 + 3) + 2xf(y) + f(x) - 3$$

, for all $x, y \in \mathbb{R}$.

Solution (by pco). Let $P(x, y)$ be the assertion

$$f(x + f(y)) = f(y^2 + 3) + 2xf(y) + f(x) - 3.$$

Note that $f \equiv 0$ is not a solution and so there exist $u, v \in \mathbb{R}$ such that $f(u) = v \neq 0$. Now, by computing

$$P\left(\frac{x + 3 - f(u^2 + 3)}{2v}, u\right),$$

we find that

$$f\left(\frac{x+3-f(u^2+3)}{2v}+v\right) - f\left(\frac{x+3-f(u^2+3)}{2v}\right) = x.$$

So, any real x may be written as a difference $x = f(a) - f(b)$ for some a, b. Notice that $P(x - f(z), z)$ gives

$$f(x) = f(z^2+3) + 2(x - f(z))f(z) + f(x - f(z)) - 3, \qquad (4.12)$$

and $P(x - f(z), y)$ implies

$$f(x + f(y) - f(z)) = f(y^2+3) + 2(x - f(z))f(y) + f(x - f(z)) - 3. \qquad (4.13)$$

Subtracting the equation in (4.12) from the one in (4.13), we get

$$f(x + f(y) - f(z)) = f(x) + f(y^2+3) - f(z^2+3) + 2xf(y) \\ - 2f(y)f(z) - 2xf(z) + 2f(z)^2.$$

Swapping y and z and adding the equations in (4.12) and (4.13), we get

$$f(x + f(y) - f(z)) + f(x + f(z) - f(y)) = 2f(x) + 2(f(y) - f(z))^2.$$

Since any real may be written as a difference $f(a) - f(b)$, this forms a new assertion which we call $Q(x, y)$:

$$f(x + y) + f(x - y) = 2f(x) + 2y^2, \quad \forall x, y \in \mathbb{R}.$$

Setting there $f(x) = g(x) + x^2$, this becomes

$$g(x + y) + g(x - y) = 2g(x).$$

This immediately implies that $g(x) - g(0)$ is additive and so, $g(x) = a(x) + b$, where $a(x)$ is any additive function and b is any real number. Therefore, $f(x) = x^2 + a(x) + b$. It remains to check constraints over $a(x)$ and b and this may be very very ugly (avoid directly plugging this value in the original equation).

    The simplest way I can think of to show that $a(x) = 0$ for all x is the following: By $P(-f(-x), x)$, we find

$$f(f(x) - f(-x)) = f(x^2+3) - 2f(x)f(-x) + f(-f(-x)) - 3,$$

and using $P(-f(-x), -x)$, we get

$$f(0) = f(x^2 + 3) - 2f(-x)^2 + f(-f(-x)) - 3.$$

Subtracting, we find

$$f(f(x) - f(-x)) = 2f(-x)(f(-x) - f(x)) + f(0).$$

Setting there $f(x) = x^2 + a(x) + b$, so that $f(x) - f(-x) = 2a(x)$, the previous equation becomes

$$f(2a(x)) = b - 4a(x)f(-x).$$

Hence, $a(a(x)) = -2(x^2 + b)a(x)$. Using the previous property and writing

$$a(a(x + y)) = a(a(x)) + a(a(y)),$$

we get

$$a(x)(2xy + y^2) + a(y)(x^2 + 2xy) = 0, \quad \forall x, y \in \mathbb{R}.$$

Just plug there $y = -2x$ and you get $a \equiv 0$. Plugging then $f(x) = x^2 + b$ in the original equation, we get $b = 3$ and so, the only solution is

$$f(x) = x^2 + 3, \quad \forall x \in \mathbb{R}.$$

Problem 84. Find all functions $f : \mathbb{R} \to \mathbb{R}$ that satisfy

$$f(x - f(y)) = f(x + y^{2016}) + 2016$$

for all reals x, y.

Solution (by pco). For easier writing, let $n = 2016$. Let $P(x, y)$ be the assertion

$$f(x - f(y)) = f(x + y^n) + n.$$

Let

$$A = \{f(x) + x^n : \forall x \in \mathbb{R}\}.$$

Then, $P(x - y^n, y)$ implies $f(x - a) = f(x) + n$ for all $x \in \mathbb{R}$ and all $a \in A$. Therefore, $f(x + b - a) = f(x)$ for all $x \in \mathbb{R}$ and all $a, b \in A$.

1. If $|A| > 1$, let $a < b \in A$ and $\Delta = b - a$. Since $f(x + \Delta) = f(x)$, both $x^n + f(x)$ and $(x + \Delta)^n + f(x)$ belong to A. Since n is even and positive, the equation

$$((x + \Delta)^n + f(x)) - (x^n + f(x)) = t$$

always has a solution. So, $b - a$ can take any value we want and so

$$f(x + t) = f(x), \quad \forall x, t \in \mathbb{R}.$$

Therefore, $f(x)$ is constant, which is not a valid solution.

2. If $|A| = 1$, then $f(x) + x^n = c$ and so

$$f(x) = c - x^n, \forall x \in \mathbb{R},$$

for some real c. Plugging this back in original equation, we get no solution in this case.

So, there are no solutions for this functional equation.

Problem 86. Let α be a fixed real number. Find all functions $f : \mathbb{R} \to \mathbb{R}$ such that

$$f(f(x+y)f(x-y)) = x^2 + \alpha y f(y)$$

for all $x, y \in \mathbb{R}$.

Solution (by pco). Let $P(x, y)$ be the assertion

$$f(f(x+y)f(x-y)) = x^2 + \alpha y f(y).$$

Plugging $P(x, 0)$ implies $f(f(x)^2) = x^2$ and so $f(a) = f(b)$ gives $a^2 = b^2$. Therefore,

$$f(f(x)^2)) = f(f(-x)^2)$$

and so $f(x)^4 = f(-x)^4$. Hence, $f(-x) = \pm f(x)$ for all real x. Now, $P(0, x)$ yields

$$f(f(x)f(-x)) = \alpha x f(x).$$

Since $f(-x) = \pm f(x)$, we find that

$$f(f(x)f(-x)) = f(\pm f(x)^2) = \pm f(f(x)^2) = \pm x^2.$$

Therefore,

$$\alpha x f(x) = \pm x^2, \quad \forall x \in \mathbb{R}.$$

This implies $\alpha \neq 0$ (there is no solution otherwise) and $f(x) = \pm x/\alpha$ for all $x \neq 0$. Plugging this in $f(f(x)^2) = x^2$, we get $\alpha \in \{-1, +1\}$. Since $\alpha \neq 0$, comparing $P(0, x)$ with $P(0, -x)$, we get

$$f(-x) = -f(x), \quad \forall x \neq 0.$$

So, $f(x) = \pm x$ for all non-zero x and $f(f(0)^2) = 0$ implies $f(0) = 0$. Considering now $f(-x) = -f(x)$ for all x (including zero), we get

$$P(0, x) \implies \alpha x f(x) = f(f(x)f(-x)) = -f(f(x)^2) = -x^2,$$

and so $f(x) = -\alpha x$ for all real x. We can check that if $\alpha = 1$, $f(x) = -\alpha x$ does not work. Hence, the only solution happens for the case when $\alpha = -1$, in which case $f(x) = -\alpha x$. One can easily check that this is indeed a solution.

Problem 87. Find all functions $f : \mathbb{R} \to \mathbb{R}$ satisfying the following condition

$$(f(x))^2 + 2f(y-x)f(-y) = (f(-x))^2 + 2f(x-y)f(y),$$

for all $x, y \in \mathbb{R}$.

Solution (by pco). Let $P(x,y)$ be the assertion

$$f(x)^2 + 2f(y-x)f(-y) = f(-x)^2 + 2f(x-y)f(y).$$

Let $a = f(0)$. Then $P(x,0)$ yields

$$(f(x) - f(-x))(f(x) + f(-x) - 2a) = 0,$$

and so for all x, either $f(-x) = f(x)$ or $f(-x) = 2a - f(x)$.

1. If $a = 0$, since $f(-x) = \pm f(x)$ for all x, $P(x+y, y)$ implies $f(-x)f(-y) = f(x)f(y)$ and so either $f(-x) = f(x)\ \forall x$ or $f(-x) = -f(x)\ \forall x$. Therefore, any odd function or any even function $f(0) = 0$. One can easily check that these both fit the original equation.

2. If $a \neq 0$, note that any even function with $f(0) \neq 0$ is also a solution. So let us from now look only for solutions where there exists some u such that $f(-u) \neq f(u)$. Define

$$U = \{x \in \mathbb{R} : f(-x) \neq f(x)\},$$
$$V = \{x \in \mathbb{R} : f(-x) = f(x)\}.$$

Some simple properties:

- $U \neq \emptyset$ (by hypothesis in this part of the solution).
- $V \neq \emptyset$ (since $0 \in V$).
- $\forall u \in U$: $-u \in U$ and $f(-u) = 2a - f(u)$ and $f(u) \neq a$ (else $f(-u) = a = f(u)$).
- $\forall v \in V$: $-v \in V$.

Take $u \in U$ and $v \in V$. Then,

$$P(u, v) \implies f(v)(f(v-u) - f(u-v)) = 2a(a - f(u)) \neq 0.$$

This implies $f(v) \neq 0$ and $u - v \in U$, and so $f(u-v) = 2a - f(v-u)$. Therefore,

$$f(v)(f(v-u) - a) = a(a - f(u)).$$

Replacing now u by $v - u \in U$, we get:

$$f(v)(f(u) - a) = a(a - f(v - u)).$$

Subtracting these two lines, this becomes

$$(f(v) - a)(f(v - u) - f(u)) = 0.$$

Hence,

- Either $f(v) = a$ and then $f(v - u) + f(u) = 2a$ and so $f(u - v) = f(u)$, or
- $f(v - u) = f(u)$ and then $f(v) = -a$.

Consider then $u \in U$ and $v \in V$ (and so $u - v \in U$).

$$P(v, u) \implies f(u - v)f(-u) = f(v - u)f(u).$$

The latter equation is

$$f(u - v)(2a - f(u)) = (2a - f(u - v))f(u).$$

Thus, $f(u - v) = f(u)$. Back four lines above, this implies $f(v) = a$ for all $v \in V$ and $f(u - v) = f(u)$ for all $u \in U$ and $v \in V$. We know that $u - v \in U$ for any $u \in U$ and any $v \in V$, and so:

$$v_1 + v_2 \in V, \quad \forall v_1, v_2 \in V.$$

Synthesis at this point:

- $u - v \in U$.
- $v - 1 + v_2 \in V$.
- $f(v) = a$.
- $f(u - v) = f(u)$.

We already checked that these properties make $P(u, v)$ and $P(v, u)$ true. It is immediate to check that $P(v_1, v_2)$ is also true and so it remains to check $P(u_1, u_2)$. Let $u_1, u_2 \in U$. Then,

$$P(u_1, u_2) \implies f(u_2 - u_1)(2a - f(u_2)) = 2a^2 - 2af(u_1) + f(u_1 - u_2)f(u_2).$$

Then,

- If $u_1 - u_2 \in V$, this becomes $f(u_1) = f(u_2)$.
- If $u_1 - u_2 \in U$, this becomes $f(u_1 - u_2) = f(u_1) - f(u_2) + a$.

Note that all the above properties imply

$$f(x) - a = 0, \quad \forall x \in V$$

and

$$f(x + y) - a = f(x) - a + f(y) - a, \quad \forall x, y \in \mathbb{R}.$$

Thus, the last set of solutions is

$$f(x) = a(x) + a, \quad \forall x \in \mathbb{R},$$

where $a(x)$ is any additive function. One can easily check that this fits the original equation.

Problem 88. For each real number t let $g(t)$ be the total number of functions $f : \mathbb{R} \to \mathbb{R}$ satisfying

$$f(xy + f(y)) = f(x)y + t$$

for all real numbers x, y. Determine the function $g(t)$.

Solution (by pco). Let $P(x, y)$ be the assertion

$$f(xy + f(y)) = f(x)y + t.$$

Define $a = f(0)$. Then, $P(x, 0)$ gives $f(a) = t$. We have a case work here.

1. If $a \neq 0$, then
$$P(0, x) \implies f(f(x)) = ax + t$$
and so f is bijective.This means that there is some $u \in \mathbb{R}$ such that $f(u) = 0$. Then, $P(u, x)$ implies $f(ux + f(x)) = t$ ans since f is injective, $ux + f(x)$ is constant. Therefore, $f(x) = c - ux$ for some $c, u \in \mathbb{R}$. Plugging this back in the original equation, we get $c = u^2$ and $u^3 - u^2 + t = 0$ with $u \neq 0$ (since $f(0) = 0$). Hence,

   - If $t > \frac{4}{27}$: one solution.
   - If $t = \frac{4}{27}$: two solutions.
   - If $0 < t < \frac{4}{27}$: three solutions.
   - If $t = 0$: one solution $u = 1$ (since $u \neq 0$).

- If $t < 0$: one solution.

2. If $a = 0$, $f(a) = t$ implies $t = 0$. Then, $f(x) = 0$ for all x is a solution. If $f(u) = v \neq 0$ for some $u, v \in \mathbb{R}$,

$$P(u, x) \implies f(ux + v) = vx,$$

and so $f(x)$ is surjective. But then $P(0, x)$ gives $f(f(x)) = 0$ and so, by surjectivity, $f \equiv 0$, contradiction.

Hence the answer is:

$$g(t) = \begin{cases} 1, & \text{if } t < 0, \\ 2, & \text{if } t = 0, \\ 3, & \text{if } 0 < t < \frac{4}{27}, \\ 2, & \text{if } t = \frac{4}{27}, \\ 1, & \text{if } t > \frac{4}{27}. \end{cases}$$

Problem 90. Do there exist functions $f, g : \mathbb{R} \to \mathbb{R}$ such that

$$f(x + f(y)) = \{y\} + g(x)$$

holds for all real x and y? Here, $\{y\}$ is the fractional part of y. That is, $\{y\} = y - \lfloor y \rfloor$.

Solution (by pco). Let $P(x, y)$ be the assertion

$$f(x + f(y)) = \{y\} + g(x).$$

Let $a = f(1)$. Then, $P(x, 1)$ implies $g(x) = f(x + a)$ and so we define the new assertion $Q(x, y)$ as

$$f(x + f(y)) = \{y\} + f(x + a).$$

For any $t \in [0, 1)$, $Q(x - a, t)$ yields

$$f(x - a + f(t)) = f(x) + t,$$

and $Q(x - f(t), t)$ implies

$$f(x - f(t) + a) = f(x) - t.$$

Therefore, $y \in f(\mathbb{R})$ implies $(y - 1, y + 1) \subset f(\mathbb{R})$. Hence, $f(x)$ is surjective. But then, $Q(a, x)$ gives

$$f(a + f(x)) = \{x\} + f(2a),$$

and so
$$f(f(x) + a) \in [f(2a), f(2a) + 1), \quad \forall x \in \mathbb{R}.$$

Now, since f is surjective, we get $f(x) \in [f(2a), f(2a) + 1)$ for all real x, which is in contradiction with the fact that $f(x)$ is surjective. Thus, no such function exists.

Problem 92. Let a be a fixed real number. Find all functions $f : \mathbb{R} \to \mathbb{R}$ such that
$$f(xy + f(y)) = f(x)y + a$$

holds for every $x, y \in \mathbb{R}$.

Solution (by pco). Let $P(x, y)$ be the assertion
$$f(xy + f(y)) = f(x)y + a.$$

Define $b = f(0)$ and $c = f(1)$.

1. If $b \neq 0$, then

$$\begin{array}{lll} P(0, x) \implies f(f(x)) = bx + a & & \implies f \text{ is bijective,} \\ P(x, f(1)) \implies f(cx + b + a) = cf(x) + a, & & \\ P(1, f(x)) \implies f(f(x) + bx + a) = cf(x) + a. & & \end{array}$$

Therefore,
$$f(cx + b + a) = f(f(x) + bx + a),$$

and so, since f is injective, we get $f(x) = (c - b)x + b$. Plugging $f(x) = ux + v$ in the original equation, we get
$$v = u^2 \text{ and } a = u^3 + u^2.$$

Hence, a first family of solutions is
$$f(x) = ux + u^2, \quad \forall x \in \mathbb{R},$$

where u is any nonzero root of the cubic $x^3 + x^2 - a = 0$

2. If $b = 0$, then

$$\begin{array}{ll} P(x, 0) \implies a = 0, \\ P(0, x) \implies f(f(x)) = 0. \end{array}$$

Suppose now that there exists $t \in \mathbb{R}$ such that $f(t) \neq 0$. Then, $P(t, x)$ implies

$$f(tx + f(x)) = f(t)x,$$

and so $f(x)$ is surjective. Let then x be a number such that $f(x) = t - f(1)$ (which exists since f is surjective). Then, using $P(f(x), 1)$, we find that $f(t) = f(f(x)) = 0$, which is impossible. Thus, $a = 0$ and the solution in this case is

$$f(x) = 0, \quad \forall x \in \mathbb{R}.$$

Problem 93. Is there a function $f : \mathbb{R} \to \mathbb{R}$ such that $f(f(x)) = x^2 + x + 3$ holds for all real x?

Solution (by pco). The answer is yes. We are going to build an infinite family of solutions for $f(x)$. Let $a \in (0, \frac{13}{4})$ and define the sequence $\{a_n\}$ by $a_0 = 0$, $a_1 = a$, and

$$a_{n+2} = a_n^2 + \frac{13}{4}, \quad \forall n \geq 0.$$

Then, a_n is an increasing sequence with limit $+\infty$. Let $h : [a_0, a_1] \to [a_1, a_2]$ be any continuous increasing bijective function. Define the sequence of functions $\{h_n(x)\}$ so that $h_n : [a_n, a_{n+1}] \to [a_{n+1}, a_{n+2}]$ is a continuous increasing bijective function, $h_0(x) = h(x)$, and for all $n \geq 0$,

$$h_{n+1}(x) = \left(h_n^{-1}(x)\right)^2 + \frac{13}{4}.$$

It is easy to check that all these finctions indeed are continuous, increasing, and bijective, and also

$$h_{n+1}(h_n(x)) = x^2 + \frac{13}{4}.$$

It remains to define $f(x)$ as

$$f(x) = h_n(|x|), \quad \text{for all } x \text{ such that } |x| \in [a_n, a_{n+1}).$$

It is easy to check that this function indeed matches all the requirements (and is also continuous).

Problem 94. Find all functions $f : \mathbb{R} \to \mathbb{R}$ such that for all reals x,

$$f(x + 2) - 2f(x + 1) + f(x) = x^2.$$

Solution (by pco). In this kind of equation, the simplest way is to find one unique solution $a(x)$ and to write $f(x) = a(x) + b(x)$ and solve the new equation.

1. Finding one solution is rather simple if we are looking only for a polynomial solution. It is easy to find for example

$$a(x) = \frac{x^4 - 4x^3 + 5x^2}{12}.$$

2. Writing then $f(x) = a(x) + b(x)$, the equation becomes

$$b(x + 2) - 2b(x + 1) + b(x) = 0.$$

This means

$$b(x + 2) - b(x + 1) = b(x + 1) - b(x)$$

and so $b(x+1) - b(x)$ is periodic with period at least 1, and one general form for all these periodic functions is $c(\{x\})$. Hence,

$$b(x + 1) = b(x) + c(\{x\}).$$

The latter equation can be written as

$$b(x + n) = b(x) + nc(\{x\})$$

for all integers $n \geq 1$. Thus,

$$b(x) = b(\{x\}) + \lfloor x \rfloor c(\{x\}),$$

and since $y = \lfloor y \rfloor + \{y\}$,

$$b(x) = xc(\{x\}) + b(\{x\}) - \{x\}c(\{x\}).$$

3. The above calculations show that

$$b(x) = xg(\{x\}) + h(\{x\})$$

holds for some $f, g : [0, 1) \to \mathbb{R}$. It is easy to check that this mandatory form indeed is enough and so is a general solution.

Therefore, the general solutions to this functional equation have the form

$$f(x) = \frac{x^4 - 4x^3 + 5x^2}{12} + xg(\{x\}) + h(\{x\}),$$

whatever are functions $g, h : [0, 1) \to \mathbb{R}$.

Problem 96. Determine all functions $f : \mathbb{R} \to \mathbb{R}$ that satisfy

$$f(x^2 + f(y)) = f(f(x)) + 2f(xy) + f(y^2)$$

for all $x, y \in \mathbb{R}$.

Solution (by pco). Let $P(x, y)$ be the assertion

$$f(x^2 + f(y)) = f(f(x)) + 2f(xy) + f(y^2).$$

$$P(0,0) \implies f(0) = 0,$$
$$P(x,0) \implies f(x^2) = f(f(x)),$$
$$P(x,y) - P(y,x) \implies f(x^2 + f(y)) = f(y^2 + f(x)),$$
$$P(x,1) - P(-x,1) \implies f(-x) = f(x).$$

If $f(a) = f(b)$, then $P(x, a) - P(x, b)$ implies $f(ax) = f(bx)$ for all x. This implies also that if $f(a) = 0$ for some $a \neq 0$, then $f \equiv 0$, which indeed is a solution. So let us from now consider

$$f(x) = 0 \iff x = 0.$$

Let then

$$U = \{u \in \mathbb{R} : f(ux) = f(x), \quad \forall x\}.$$

Then U is a multiplicative group containing 1 and -1. We also previously got $f(a) = f(b) \neq 0$ implies $\frac{a}{b} \in U$.

1. If $U = \{-1, 1\}$, consider any real $x \neq 0$. Then, $f(f(x)) = f(x^2)$ implies $\frac{f(x)}{x^2} \in U$, and so for all x, either $f(x) = x^2$ or $f(x) = -x^2$. If there exist $x, y \neq 0$ such that $f(x) = x^2$ and $f(y) = -y^2$, then

$$f(x^2 + f(y)) = f(y^2 + f(x)) \implies (x^2 - y^2) = \pm(x^2 + y^2),$$

which is impossible. So, either $f(x) = x^2$ for all x, which is a valid solution, or $f(x) = -x^2$ for all x, which is not a solution if we plug it in the priginal equation.

2. If there exists $u \in U \setminus \{-1, 1\}$, then

   - **Claim.** There exists x such that $f(x) < 0$.
     Proof: WLOG suppose that $u > 0$. Then, $u^n \in U$ for all $n \in \mathbb{Z}$. Let then $x, y > 0$. We can choose $n \in \mathbb{Z}$ such that $u^n y^2 > f(y)$ and so

   $$P(\sqrt{u^n y^2 - f(y)}, y) \implies f(u^n y^2 - f(y)) + 2f(\sqrt{u^n y^2 - f(y)}\,y) = 0.$$

   So, one of the two summands is less than 0.

- **Claim.** No such function exists.

  Proof: Let x be such that $f(x) < 0$. Then

  $$f(x^2 + f(\sqrt{-f(x)})) = f((\sqrt{-f(x)})^2 + f(x)) = 0,$$

  and so $f(\sqrt{-f(x)}) = -x^2$. But ux is defined such that $f(ux) = f(x) < 0$, and so $f(\sqrt{-f(ux)}) = -u^2 x^2$, which means $u^2 = 1$, impossible.

Substitutions

Problem 100. Find all functions $f : \mathbb{R} \to \mathbb{R}$ such that

$$(a - b)f(a + b) + (b - c)f(b + c) + (c - a)f(c + a) = 0$$

for all $a, b, c \in \mathbb{R}$.

Solution (by pco). Let $P(x, y, z)$ be the assertion

$$(x - y)f(x + y) + (y - z)f(y + z) + (z - x)f(z + x) = 0.$$

Notice that

$$P\left(\frac{x + 1}{2}, \frac{x - 1}{2}, \frac{1 - x}{2}\right) \implies f(x) = x(f(1) - f(0)) + f(0),$$

and so

$$f(x) = ax + b, \quad \forall x \in \mathbb{R},$$

which indeed is a solution for any choice of $a, b \in \mathbb{R}$.

Problem 101. Find al functions $f : \mathbb{R} \to \mathbb{R}$ such that for all reals x and y, we have $f(x + y) = f(x) + f(y)$ and $f(x^3) = x^2 f(x)$.

Solution (by pco). Let $k \in \mathbb{Q}$ be arbitrary. Write $f((x + k)^3) = (x + k)^2 f(x + k)$, which expands to

$$f(x^3) + 3kf(x^2) + 3k^2 f(x) + k^3 f(1) = (x^2 + 2kx + k^2)(f(x) + kf(1)).$$

This then simplifies to

$$2k^2(f(x) - xf(1)) + k(3f(x^2) - 2xf(x) - x^2 f(1)) = 0.$$

The latter is a polynomial (in k) with infinitely many roots (any rational number) and so this is the all-zero polynomial and all its coefficients are zero. Looking at the coefficient of k^2, this gives $f(x) = ax$ for all x, which indeed is a solution, whatever is $a = f(1) \in \mathbb{R}$.

Problem 103. Find all functions $f : \mathbb{R} \to \mathbb{R}$ such that $f(x)f(xf(y)) = x^2 f(y)$ holds for all $x, y \in \mathbb{R}$.

Solution (by pco). $f(x) = 0$ for all x is a solution. So, from now on, let's look only for non-all-zero solutions. Let $P(x, y)$ be the assertion

$$f(x)f(xf(y)) = x^2 f(y).$$

Let $u, v \in \mathbb{R}$ be such that $f(u) = v \neq 0$. Also, assume that $a = f(1)$.

$P(0, 0)$ implies $f(0) = 0$. If $f(t) = 0$ for some $t \neq 0$, then $P(t, u)$ yields $v = 0$, which is impossible. Therefore,

$$f(x) = 0 \iff x = 0$$

and so $a \neq 0$. Let x be any real number such that $vx > 0$. Now,

$$P\left(\sqrt{\frac{x}{v}}, u\right) \implies f\left(\sqrt{\frac{x}{v}}\right) f\left(v\sqrt{\frac{x}{v}}\right) = x$$

Hence, any nonzero real x with same sign as v may be written as $x = f(w)f(t)$ for some non-zero reals w, t. Consider such an x and suppose that $x = f(w)f(t)$. Then,

$$P(1, w) \implies f(f(w)) = \frac{f(w)}{a}$$

and

$$P(f(w), t) \implies f(f(w)f(t)) = af(w)f(t), \quad \forall w, t \neq 0$$

Therefore, $f(x) = ax$ for any nonzero x with same sign as v.

Obviously, if there exists $u' \neq 0$ such that $f(u') = v'$, where v' has opposite sign from c, the same path leads to $f(x) = ax$ for any nonzero x with same sign as v' and so $f(x) = ax$ for all x. Plugging this back in original equation, we get $a^2 = 1$ and thus

$$f(x) = x, \quad \forall x \in \mathbb{R}$$

and

$$f(x) = -x, \quad \forall x \in \mathbb{R}$$

are the only solutions in tis case.

On the other hand, if $f(x)$ has a constant sign, then it must be positive since $f(x) = ax$ holds for all real x and $f(x)$ and a both have same sign. Summarizing, $f(x) > 0$ for all $x \neq 0$ and $f(x) = ax$ for all $x \geq 0$. From

$$f(f(x)) = \frac{1}{a}f(x)$$

we then get $a = 1$, and $P(x, 1)$ yields $f(x)^2 = x^2$. Hence, since $f(x) > 0, \forall x \neq 0$, we find that

$$f(x) = |x|, \quad \forall x \in \mathbb{R},$$

which indeed is a solution.

Problem 104. Find all funtions $f : \mathbb{R} \to \mathbb{R}$ such that for all $x, y \in \mathbb{R}$, we have

$$f(f(x+y)) = f(x+y) + f(x)f(y) - xy.$$

Solution (by pco). Let $f(0) = a$ and show that $af(x+y) = f(x)f(y) - xy$ holds for all x and y. If $a \neq 0$,

$$f(x + y) = \frac{1}{a}f(x)f(y) - \frac{1}{a}xy.$$

Use change of variables $y \mapsto y + z$ to obtain

$$f(x + y + z) = \frac{1}{a^2}f(x)f(y)f(z) - \frac{1}{a^2}xyf(z) - \frac{1}{a}xz - \frac{1}{a}yz.$$

Swapping y and z and subtracting, conclude that f must be linear, so that $f(x) = cx + a$. Plug it back in the original equation to see it doesn't work. So, $a = 0$ and $f(x) = x$ for all x is the only solution that works in this case.

Problem 105. Find all functions $f : \mathbb{R} \to \mathbb{R}$ such that

$$f(xf(y)) = (1 - y)f(xy) + x^2y^2 f(y)$$

holds for all reals x and y.

Solution (by pco). Let $P(x, y)$ be the assertion

$$f(xf(y)) = (1 - y)f(xy) + x^2y^2 f(y).$$

By $P(0, 1)$ we find $f(0) = 0$. If $f(1) \neq 0$,

$$P\left(\frac{x}{f(1)}, 1\right) \implies f(x) = \frac{x^2}{f(1)}, \quad \forall x \in \mathbb{R},$$

which is never a solution. So, $f(1) = 0$. If $f(u) = 0$ for some $u \notin \{0, 1\}$, then:

$$P\left(\frac{x}{u}, u\right) \implies f(x) = 0, \quad \forall x \in \mathbb{R},$$

which indeed is a solution. So, let us consider from now that

$$f(x) = 0 \iff x \in \{0, 1\}.$$

By $P(1, x)$, we find $f(f(x)) = (x^2 - x + 1)f(x)$ and this means that $f(a) = f(b)$ for $a, b \notin \{0, 1\}$ implies either $a = b$ or $a + b = 1$. Let $x \notin \{0, 1\}$. Then,

$$P\left(\frac{1}{x}, x\right) \implies f\left(\frac{f(x)}{x}\right) = f(x),$$

and hence either

$$\frac{f(x)}{x} = x \implies f(x) = x^2,$$

or

$$\frac{f(x)}{x} + x = 1 \implies f(x) = x - x^2.$$

Let then $x \notin \{0, \frac{1}{2}, 1\}$ such that $f(x) = x^2$. Using $P(1, x)$, we get

$$f(x^2) = (x^2 - x + 1)x^2$$

and so either

$$f(x^2) = x^4 \implies x^4 = (x^2 - x + 1)x^2,$$

or

$$f(x^2) = x^2 - x^4 \implies x^2 - x^4 = (x^2 - x + 1)x^2.$$

Both of these are impossible. Thus, the non-trivial solution is $f(x) = x - x^2$ for all x, which is actually a solution to the initial functional equation.

Problem 106. Find all functions $f : \mathbb{R} \to \mathbb{R}$ such that

$$f(x + y) = f(x) + f(y) + f(xy)$$

for all $x, y \in \mathbb{R}$.

Solution (by pco). Let $P(x, y)$ be the given assertion and let $a = f(1)$. Note that $P(0, 0)$ implies $f(0) = 0$ and $P(x, 1)$ gives $f(x + 1) = 2f(x) + a$. Moreover, $P(x, y + 1)$ yields

$$2f(x + y) + a = f(x) + 2f(y) + a + f(xy + x).$$

Therefore,

$$2(f(x) + f(y) + f(xy)) = f(x) + 2f(y) + f(xy + x),$$

which can be reduced to $f(xy + x) = f(x) + 2f(xy)$.

Setting $y \to \frac{y}{x}$ in the last equation, we find $f(x + y) = f(x) + 2f(y)$ for all reals x and y with $y \neq 0$. Swapping x, y and subtracting, we get $f(x) = f(y) = c$ for all $x, y \neq 0$, where c is a constant. Then $P(1, -1)$ would easily give us $c = 0$.

So, $f \equiv 0$, which indeed is a solution.

Problem 107. Find all functions $f : \mathbb{R} \to \mathbb{R}$ such that

$$f(x^3) - f(y^3) = (x^2 + xy + y^2)(f(x) - f(y)).$$

Solution (by pco). Let $P(x, y)$ be the given assertion. If $f(x)$ is a solution then so is $f(x) + c$. So, WLOG, suppose that $f(0) = 0$. Now $P(x, 0)$ implies $f(x^3) = x^2 f(x)$ and therefore $P(x, y)$ may be written as

$$x^2 f(x) - y^2 f(y) = (x^2 + xy + y^2)(f(x) - f(y)).$$

This is $y(x + y)f(x) = x(x + y)f(y)$, and hence

$$\frac{f(x)}{x} = \frac{f(y)}{y}$$

for all reals x and y such that $x, y, x + y \neq 0$. Then trivially $f(x) = ax$ and so the solution is

$$f(x) = ax + b, \quad \forall x \in \mathbb{R},$$

which indeed is a solution, whatever are $a, b \in \mathbb{R}$.

Problem 108. Find all functions $f : \mathbb{R} \to \mathbb{R}$ satisfying

$$f\left(f\left(x + f\left(y\right)\right) - y - f\left(x\right)\right) = xf\left(y\right) - yf\left(x\right)$$

for all real numbers x, y.

Solution (by Murad Aghazade). Let $P(x, y)$ be the given functional equation. Firstly, $P(x, x)$ yields that there exists $a \in \mathbb{R}$ such that $f(a) = 0$. Then $P(x, a)$ gives that either $a = 0$ or f is constant. If f is constant, it must be zero. If $a = 0$, then $P(0, x)$ yields $f(f(x)) = x$. Now,

$$P(f(x), -x) \implies f(x) + f(-x) = f(x)f(-x) + x^2 \tag{4.14}$$
$$P(x, f(-x)) \implies f(-f(x) - f(-x)) = -f(x) - f(-x).$$

The key pluggings are

$$P(-x, x + f(x)) \implies (x + f(x))(-x - f(-x)) = -(f(x) + f(-x)).$$

By (4.14), we easily get f is odd because we got $(x + f(x))(-x - f(-x)) = -(f(x) + f(-x))$ but we also have $f(x) + f(-x) = f(x)f(-x) + x^2$, and this easily implies $f(x) = -f(-x)$.

Finally, $P(x + f(x), -x)$ gives $f(x) \in x, -x$. In the case when there exist $a, b \neq 0$ such that $f(a) = a$ and $f(b) = -b$, use $P(a, f(b))$ to get a contradiction. It remains to check all the solutions and see they actually work:

- $f \equiv 0$.

- $f(x) = x$ for all x.

- $f(x) = -x$ for all x.

Problem 109. Find all functions $f : \mathbb{R} \to \mathbb{R}$ such that

$$f(f(x+y) - x) f(f(x+y) - y) = xy$$

holds for all $x, y \in \mathbb{R}$.

Solution (by pco). Let $P(x, y)$ be the assertion. If there exists u such that $f(u) = 0$, then

$$P(-u, 2u) \implies u = 0, \qquad P(x, 0) \implies f(f(x) - x)f(f(x)) = 0,$$

and so either $f(x) = x$, or $x = 0$ and $f(0) = 0$. Therefore, $f(x) = x$ for all x, which indeed is a solution.

Problem 110. Find all functions $f : \mathbb{R} \to \mathbb{R}$ such that

$$(y+1)f(x) + f(xf(y) + f(x+y)) = y$$

for all $x, y \in \mathbb{R}$.

Solution (by ThE-dArK-lOrD). As usual, let $P(x, y)$ denote

$$(y+1)f(x) + f(xf(y) + f(x+y)) = y$$

for all $x, y \in \mathbb{R}$. Note that $P(0, y)$ gives us

$$f(f(y)) = y(1 - f(0)) - f(0),$$

for all $y \in \mathbb{R}$. There are two possible cases for $1 - f(0)$:

1. If $1 - f(0) \neq 0$, we get that f is injective. Now, $P(x, -1)$ implies

$$f(xf(-1) + f(x-1)) = -1$$

for all $x \in \mathbb{R}$. By injectivity, there exists a real constant c that $f(x-1) + xf(-1) = c$ for all $x \in \mathbb{R}$. In other words, f is a linear function. Plugging in the initial condition, we easily find that the only one possible solution in this case is $f(x) = -x$ for all $x \in \mathbb{R}$.

2. If $1 - f(0) = 0$, then we get that $f(f(y)) = -f(0)$ for all $y \in \mathbb{R}$. Note that $1 + f(0) = 2 \neq 0$. Now, $P(f(x), y)$ yields

$$(y + 1)(-f(0)) + f(f(x)f(y) + f(f(x) + y)) = y$$

for all $x, y \in \mathbb{R}$. Hence,

$$f(f(x)f(y) + f(f(x) + y)) = y(1 + f(0)) + f(0),$$

and so $-f(0) = f(y(1+f(0))+f(0))$ for all $x, y \in \mathbb{R}$. Since $1+f(0) \neq 0$, when y varies over $\mathbb{R}$, $y(1+f(0))+f(0)$ can take any real number as its value. Hence, f must be a constant function. Plugging in the initial condition gives no possible solution in this case.

Therefore, the only solution to this problem is $f(x) = -x$ for all $x \in \mathbb{R}$.

Problem 111. Find all functions $f : \mathbb{R} \to \mathbb{R}$ for which

$$f(x - f(y)) = f(x) - \lfloor y \rfloor$$

for all reals x, y.

Solution (by pco). Let $P(x, y)$ be the given assertion. If $f(u) = f(v)$, then $P(x, u)$ versus $P(x, v)$ implies $\lfloor u \rfloor = \lfloor v \rfloor$. If $y \in [0, 1)$, then $f(x - f(y)) = f(x)$ and so $\lfloor x - f(y) \rfloor = \lfloor x \rfloor$ for all x. Therefore, $f(x) = 0$ for any $x \in [0, 1)$. Now,

$$P(f(x), x) \implies f(f(x)) = \lfloor x \rfloor$$
$$P(x, f(y)) \implies f(x - \lfloor y \rfloor) = f(x) - \lfloor f(y) \rfloor,$$

and so $0 = f(x - \lfloor x \rfloor) = f(x) - \lfloor f(x) \rfloor$, which means $f(x) \in \mathbb{Z}, \quad \forall x$. Then repeated application of $P(x, y)$ implies

$$f(x - kf(y)) = f(x) - k\lfloor y \rfloor.$$

Setting $k = f(z)$, this is

$$f(x - f(z)f(y)) = f(x) - f(z)\lfloor y \rfloor.$$

Swapping y and z:

$$f(x - f(y)f(z)) = f(x) - f(y)\lfloor z \rfloor.$$

Thus,

$$f(z)\lfloor y \rfloor = f(y)\lfloor z \rfloor.$$

This gives us $f(x) = k\lfloor x \rfloor$ for all x and for some $k \in \mathbb{Z}$. Plugging this back in original equation, we get $k^2 = 1$ and so the solutions are

- $f(x) = \lfloor x \rfloor$, and

- $f(x) = -\lfloor x \rfloor$.

Problem 112. Find all functions $f : \mathbb{R} \to \mathbb{R}$ that satisfy for all real x the equation

$$\lfloor f(x^4 - 5x^2 + 2015)^3 \rfloor + \lfloor f(x^4 - 5x^2 + 2015) \rfloor = \lfloor x^4 + x^2 + 1 \rfloor.$$

Solution (by pco). $x = 1$ implies $\lfloor f(2011)^3 \rfloor + \lfloor f(2011) \rfloor = 3$ and $x = 2$ implies $\lfloor f(2011)^3 \rfloor + \lfloor f(2011) \rfloor = 21$, which is a contradiction.

Problem 114. Find all functions $f : \mathbb{R} \to \mathbb{R}$ such that for all real numbers x and y,
$$(x + f(x)^2)f(y) = f(yf(x)) + xyf(x).$$

Solution (by pco). Let $P(x, y)$ be the given assertion and define $a = f(0)$ and $c = f(1)$. Then, $P(2, 0)$ implies $a(1 + f(2)^2) = 0$ and so $a = 0$. If $f(u) = 0$ for some $u \neq 0$, then use $P(u, x)$ to find that

$$f(x) = 0, \quad \forall x \in \mathbb{R} \tag{4.15}$$

which indeed is a solution. So let us from now consider $f(x) = 0$ if and only if $x = 0$ (note then that $c \neq 0$). Now, $P(1, 1)$ implies $f(c) = c^3$ and

$$P\left(-c^2, \frac{c}{f(-c^2)}\right) \implies f(-c^2)^2 = c^2$$
$$P\left(-c^2, \frac{x}{f(-c^2)}\right) \implies f(x) = c^2 x.$$

and so, setting there $x = 1$ gives $c = 1$ and so

$$f(x) = x, \quad \forall x \in \mathbb{R} \tag{4.16}$$

which indeed is a solution. So, the solutions are given by (4.15) and (4.16).

Problem 116. Find all functions $f : \mathbb{R} \to \mathbb{R}$ such that

$$f(xf(y) - y) + f(xy - x) + f(x + y) = 2xy$$

for all $x, y \in \mathbb{R}$.

Solution (by pco). Let $P(x, y)$ be the assertion

$$f(xf(y) - y) + f(xy - x) + f(x + y) = 2xy.$$

It is easily implied from $P(0, 0)$ that $f(0) = 0$. Also, $P(x, 0)$ implies $f(x) + f(-x) = 0$ and so $f(x)$ is odd. Now,

$$P\left(-1, \frac{1}{2}\right) \implies f(u) = -1, \text{ where } u = -f\left(\frac{1}{2}\right) - \frac{1}{2}.$$

We get from $P(x, u)$ that $f(x(u - 1)) = 2ux$. This implies $u \neq 1$ and $f(x) = ax$ for some $a = 2u/(u - 1)$. Plugging this back in the original equation, we get $a \in \{-2, 1\}$, and so, either

$$f(x) = x, \quad \forall x \in \mathbb{R},$$

or

$$f(x) = -2x, \quad \forall x \in \mathbb{R}.$$

One can easily check that these are valid solutions.

Problem 118. If f, g are non-constant functions from reals to reals that satisfy

$$f(x + y) = f(x)g(y) + g(x)f(y)$$

and

$$g(x + y) = g(x)g(y) - f(x)f(y),$$

then find all values that $f(0)$ and $g(0)$ can take.

Solution (by pco). Setting $x = y = 0$, we get $f(0) = 2f(0)g(0)$ and so either $f(0) = 0$ or $g(0) = \frac{1}{2}$. Also,

$$g(0) = g(0)^2 - f(0)^2,$$

and so

- If $f(0) = 0$, either $g(0) = 0$ or $g(0) = 1$.

- If $g(0) = \frac{1}{2}$, then $f(0)^2 = -\frac{1}{4}$, which is impossible.

So, there are two possibilities:

- $(f(0), g(0)) = (0, 0)$. But then, setting $y = 0$ in the first equation, we get $f(x) = 0 \quad \forall x$, impossible since the functions are non-constant.

- $(f(0), g(0)) = (0, 1)$. This can be reached for example when $f(x) = \sin x$ and $g(x) = \cos x$ (just the classical d'Alembert equations).

Problem 119. Find all functions $f : \mathbb{R} \to \mathbb{R}$ such that

$$f(f(xy - x)) + f(x + y) = yf(x) + f(y)$$

for all real numbers x and y.

Solution (by pco). Let $P(x, y)$ be the assertion

$$f(f(xy - x)) + f(x + y) = yf(x) + f(y).$$

Notice that $P(0, 0)$ implies $f(f(0)) = 0$ and $P(0, 1)$ implies $f(0) = 0$. Now, by $P(x - 1, 0)$, we find out

$$f(f(1 - x)) + f(x - 1) = 0,$$

and by $P(-1, x)$, we get

$$f(f(1 - x)) + f(x - 1) = xf(-1) + f(x).$$

Subtracting, we get $f(x) = ax$ for all x, where $a = -f(-1)$. Plugging this back in original equation, we get $a \in \{0, 1\}$ and the two solutions are

$$f(x) = 0, \quad \forall x \in \mathbb{R} \quad \text{and} \quad f(x) = x, \quad \forall x \in \mathbb{R}.$$

Problem 120. Determine all functions $f : \mathbb{R} \to \mathbb{R}$ satisfying

$$f(x^2 + f(x)f(y)) = xf(x + y)$$

for all real numbers x and y.

Solution (by pco). The only constant solution is $f(x) = 0, \quad \forall x$. So let us from now look only for non-constant solutions. Let $P(x, y)$ be the assertion

$$f(x^2 + f(x)f(y)) = xf(x + y).$$

If there is some u such that $f(u) = 0$, then $P(u, x-u)$ implies $f(u^2) = uf(x)$. So, $u = 0$ because otherwise $f(x) = f(u^2)/u$ is constant. Now, since $P(0, 0)$ implies $f(f(0)^2) = 0$, we get that

$$f(x) = 0 \iff x = 0.$$

Comparing $P(x, 0)$ with $P(-x, 0)$, we get $f(-x) = -f(x)$ for all x. Notice that $P(x, -x)$ yields $f(x^2 - f(x)^2) = 0$, and so

$$f(x) = \pm x, \text{ for all } x \in \mathbb{R}.$$

Suppose now that there exist $x, y \in \mathbb{R}$ such that $f(x) = x$ and $f(y) = -y$. Then, $P(x, y)$ implies $x^2 - xy = \pm(x^2 + xy)$ and this gives $xy = 0$. Hence, either $f(x) = x$ for all x, which indeed is a solution, or $f(x) = -x$ for all x, which is also a valid solution.

Problem 121. Find all functions $f : \mathbb{R} \to \mathbb{R}$ such that for any real numbers x and y,
$$f(yf(x) - xy - x) = f(x)f(y) - xf(y) + x.$$

Solution (by pco). Let $P(x, y)$ be the assertion
$$f(yf(x) - xy - x) = f(x)f(y) - xf(y) + x.$$

Note that $P(0, 0)$ gives $f(0) = f(0)^2$ and so $f(0) \in \{0, 1\}$.

1. If $f(0) = 0$, then $P(-x, 0)$ gives $f(x) = -x$ for all x, which is a valid solution.

2. If $f(0) = 1$, then $f(-x) = f(x)$ and so f is an even function. Let then u, v be reals such that $|u| \neq |v|$. Consider $x = -(u + v)/2 \neq 0$.

    - If $f(x) \neq x$, Comparing
    $$P\left(x, \frac{u - v}{2(f(x) - x)}\right) \text{ and } P\left(x, -\frac{u - v}{2(f(x) - x)}\right),$$
    we get $f(u) = f(v)$.

    - If $f(x) = x$, then $f(x) \neq -x$ and comparing
    $$P\left(-x, \frac{u - v}{2(f(x) + x)}\right) \text{ with } P\left(-x, -\frac{u - v}{2(f(x) + x)}\right),$$
    we find $f(-u) = f(-v)$, and so $f(u) = f(v)$. Therefore, f is constant and we get $f \equiv 1$, which is indeed a solution.

Problem 124. Find all functions $f : \mathbb{R} \to \mathbb{R}$ such that
$$f(f(x))f(y) - xy = f(x) + f(f(y)) - 1$$

holds for all reals x and y.

Solution (by pco). Let $P(x, y)$ be the assertion

$$f(f(x))f(y) - xy = f(x) + f(f(y)) - 1.$$

$P(y, x)$ yields

$$f(f(y))f(x) - xy = f(y) + f(f(x)) - 1.$$

Multiplying the latter equation by $f(y)$ and adding to the equation given by $P(x, y)$, we get

$$f(x)(f(f(y))f(y) - 1) = x(yf(y) + y) + f(y)^2 - f(y) + f(f(y)) - 1.$$
$$(4.17)$$

If there exists some u such that $f(f(u))f(u) \neq 1$, then set $y = u$ in (4.17) to get $f(x) = ax + b$ for some a, b depending on u. Plugging this back in the orginal equation we get that no such a, b fit. So,

$$f(f(y))f(y) = 1, \quad \forall y \in \mathbb{R}.$$

Then (4.17) becomes

$$0 = x(yf(y) + y) + f(y)^2 - f(y) + f(f(y)) - 1, \quad \forall x, y \in \mathbb{R},$$

and so $f(y) = -1$ for all $y \neq 0$ which unfortunately is not a solution. So, no such function exists.

Problem 126. Determine all functions $f : \mathbb{R} \to \mathbb{R}$ such that for all $x, y \in \mathbb{R}$

$$f(xf(y) - yf(x)) = f(xy) - xy.$$

Solution. Put $y = 0$ to get either f constant, which is absurd, or $f(0) = 0$. Put $x = y = \sqrt{t}$ for $t \geq 0$ to get $f(t) = t$ for $t \geq 0$. Now let $c = f(-1)$. Put $(x, y) = (t, -1)$ and $(x, y) = (-1, t)$ for $t < 0$ to conclude $f(-t) = -t + |t + ct| = (|1 + c| - 1)t$. Let $k = 1 - |1 + c|$.

So we just need to find all k such that the function f defined by $f(x) = x$ for $x \geq 0$ and $f(x) = kx$ for $x \leq 0$ works. Clearly it suffices to check when $xy < 0$. By cases we see that this forces $|k^2 - k| = |k - 1|$ hence $k = \pm 1$ both of which work.

Hence the answers are the identity function and the absolute value function.

Problem 127. Find all functions $f : \mathbb{R} \to \mathbb{R}$ which satisfy

$$f(x^3) + f(y^3) + f(z^3) = (x + y + z)(f^2(x) + f^2(y) + f^2(z) - xy - yz - zx)$$

for all reals x, y, z.

Solution (by pco). Let $P(x, y, z)$ be the given assertion and define $a = f(1)$. Then,

$$P(0,0,0) \implies f(0) = 0,$$
$$P(1,0,0) \implies a = a^2 \qquad\qquad \implies a \in \{0, 1\},$$
$$P(1,1,0) \implies 2a = 2(2a^2 - 1) \qquad \implies a = 1,$$
$$P(1,1,1) \implies 3a = 3(3a^2 - 3) \qquad \implies a \neq 1.$$

And so, no such function exists.

Problem 130. Find all functions $f : \mathbb{R} \to \mathbb{R}$ such that for all $x, y \in \mathbb{R}$:

$$f(x^2) + f(xy) = f(x)f(y) + yf(x) + xf(x + y).$$

Solution (by pco). Let $P(x, y)$ be the assertion

$$f(x^2) + f(xy) = f(x)f(y) + yf(x) + xf(x + y).$$

$P(0, x)$ implies $f(0)(f(x) + x - 2) = 0$.

- If $f(0) \neq 0$, this gives

$$f(x) = 2 - x, \quad \forall x \in \mathbb{R},$$

  which indeed is a solution.

- If $f(0) = 0$, then $P(x, 0)$ gives $f(x^2) = xf(x)$ and so $f(-x) = -f(x)$. Furthermore, $P(x, -x)$ implies $f(x)(f(x) + x) = 0$ and so for any $x \in \mathbb{R}$, either $f(x) = 0$ or $f(x) = -x$. Suppose then there exist $u, v \neq 0$ such that $f(u) = 0$ and $f(v) = -v$. Checking $P(u, v)$ easily yields $f(uv) = uf(u + v)$ and so $f(uv) = f(u + v) = 0$ (no other possibilities). On the other hand, $P(v, u)$ implies

$$-v^2 + f(uv) = -uv + vf(u + v),$$

  and so $u = v$, impossible. Therefore, the only solution in this case is

$$f(x) = 0, \quad \forall x \in \mathbb{R}.$$

One can check that this is a valid solution.

Problem 131. Find all functions $f : \mathbb{R} \to \mathbb{R}$ such that

$$f(f(x) + y) = f(x^2 - y) + 4yf(x), \quad \forall x, y \in \mathbb{R}.$$

Solution (by pco). Set $y = \frac{x^2 - f(x)}{2}$ in the equation and you get

$$f(x)(x^2 - f(x)) = 0,$$

and so for all x, either $f(x) = 0$ or $f(x) = x^2$. Suppose now that there exist $a, b \neq 0$ such that $f(a) = a^2$ and $f(b) = 0$. Then, $P(a, a^2 - b)$ implies

$$f(2a^2 - b) = 4(a^2 - b)a^2,$$

and hence, either

$$f(2a^2 - b) = (2a^2 - b)^2 \implies (2a^2 - b)^2 = 4(a^2 - b)a^2 \implies b = 0,$$

which is impossible, or

$$f(2a^2 - b) = 0 \implies b = a^2.$$

But $P(b, b)$ yields $f(b^2 - b) = 0$ and so either $b^2 - b = 0$ or $b^2 - b = b = a^2$. Therefore, $b \in \{0, 1, 2\}$ and $a \in \{0, 1, \sqrt{2}\}$. This is again, impossible. So either $f \equiv 0$ or $f(x) = x^2$ for all reals x. It is easy to check back that these two functions indeed are solutions.

4.3   Functions Over $\mathbb{Q}$

4.3.1   Cauchy-type and Jensen-type

Problem 133. Find all functions $f : \mathbb{Q} \setminus \{0\} \to \mathbb{Q}$ that for any $m, n \in \mathbb{Q}$ satisfy:

$$f(m + n) = \frac{1}{f\left(\frac{1}{m}\right) + f\left(\frac{1}{n}\right)}.$$

Solution (by pco). Let $P(x, y)$ be the assertion

$$f(x + y) = \frac{1}{f(\frac{1}{x}) + f(\frac{1}{y})},$$

true for all $x, y \neq 0$. Subtracting $P(x + y, z)$ from $P(x, y + z)$, we get

$$f\left(\frac{1}{x + y}\right) + f\left(\frac{1}{z}\right) = f\left(\frac{1}{x}\right) + f\left(\frac{1}{y + z}\right), \quad \forall x, y, z, x + y, y + z \neq 0.$$

Define $g : \mathbb{Q} \setminus \{0\} \to \mathbb{Q}$ as $g(x) = f(1/x)$ to get

$$g(x + y) + g(z) = g(x) + g(y + z), \quad \forall x, y, z, x + y, y + z \neq 0.$$

It is immediate from here to get $g(x+y) = g(x)+h(y)$ for some function $h : \mathbb{Q} \setminus \{0\} \to \mathbb{Q}$. Swapping x, y and subtracting, we get $h(y) = g(y) - c$ for some constant c and the equation becomes

$$g(x + y) = g(x) + g(y) - c, \quad \forall x, y, x + y \neq 0.$$

We can then easily conclude that $g(x) = ax + c$ (remember we deal with rational numbers). Therefore, $f(x) = a/x + c$. Plugging this in the original equation, we need $c = 0$ (else $c \notin \mathbb{Q}$) and $a \in \{-1, +1\}$. Therefore, the solutions are

$$f(x) = \frac{1}{x} \quad \forall x \in \mathbb{Q} \setminus \{0\},$$

and

$$f(x) = -\frac{1}{x} \quad \forall x \in \mathbb{Q} \setminus \{0\}.$$

Problem 134. Find all functions $f : \mathbb{Q} \to \mathbb{R} \setminus \{0\}$ such that

$$(f(x))^2 f(2y) + (f(y))^2 f(2x) = 2f(x)f(y)f(x + y)$$

for all $x, y \in \mathbb{Q}$.

Solution. Let $P(x,y)$ be the given assertion. If $f(x)$ is a solution, then $cf(x)$ is also a solution and so WLOG $f(0) = 1$ (since $0 \notin f(\mathbb{Q})$). Now,

$$P(x,0) \implies f(2x) = f(x)^2,$$

and $P(x,y)$ becomes $f(x+y) = f(x)f(y)$. Hence the solution is $f(x) = be^{ax}\ \forall x \in \mathbb{Q}$, which indeed is a solution, whatever constants $a \in \mathbb{R}\ b \in \mathbb{R} \backslash \{0\}$ one chooses.

4.3.2 Injective, Surjective, and Monotone Functions

Problem 135. For any function $f : \mathbb{Q}^+ \to \mathbb{Q}$ satisfying

$$f(xy) = f(x) + f(y)$$

for all $x, y \in \mathbb{Q}^+$, prove that f is not injective. Also, prove that f can be surjective.

Solution (by pco and Loppukilpailija).

- If $f(2) = 0$, then $f(2^2) = 0$ and $f(x)$ is not injective. If $f(3) = 0$, then $f(3^2) = 0$ and $f(x)$ is not injective. If $f(2) = a/b$ and $f(3) = c/d$ for some $a, b, c, d \in \mathbb{Z}^{\neq 0}$, then

$$f(2^{bc}) = f(3^{ad}) = ac$$

  and $f(x)$ is not injective.

- The cardinality of rational numbers and the prime numbers are the same. Let $p_1, p_2, \ldots$ be all the primes, and define $f(p_1), f(p_2), \ldots$ in such a way that they go through all the rational numbers. This is possible due to the cardinality. Now, for the rest of the numbers, just define

$$f(x) = f(q_1^{a_1} \cdot q_2^{a_2} \cdot \ldots \cdot q_n^{a_n}) = a_1 f(q_1) + \ldots + a_n f(q_n),$$

  where $q_1^{a_1} q_2^{a_2} \cdots q_n^{a_n}$ is the prime factorization of x. It's easy to see that this satisfies the given equation. So, f is surjective, as for all rational numbers q there is some prime p so that $f(p) = q$.

4.3.3   Functions on $\mathbb{Q}^+$

Problem 136. Find all $f : \mathbb{Q}^+ \to \mathbb{Q}^+$ such that $f(x+1) = f(x)$ and

$$f\left(\frac{1}{x}\right) = x^2 f(x)$$

for all positive rational numbers x.

Solution (by pco). If $f(x)$ is a solution then $tf(x)$ is also a solution whatever is $t \in \mathbb{Q}^+$. So, WLOG, suppose that $f(1) = 1$. Using continued fractions, it is easy to prove that if a solution exists, it must be unique. Since

$$f\left(\frac{p}{q}\right) = \left(\frac{q}{\gcd(p,q)}\right)^2$$

is a rather trivial solution, it is the unique one (with $f(1) = 1$).

   Hence the answer is

$$f\left(\frac{p}{q}\right) = k\left(\frac{q}{\gcd(p,q)}\right)^2,$$

which indeed is a solution, whatever is $k \in \mathbb{Q}^+$.

4.3.4   Miscellaneous

Problem 138. Find all functions $f : \mathbb{Q} \to \mathbb{R}$ such that

$$f(x+y) + f(x-y) = 2\max(f(x), f(y))$$

for all rationals x, y.

Solution (by pco). Let $P(x, y)$ be the assertion and $b = f(0)$. Comparing $P(x, y)$ with $P(y, x)$, we get that $f(x)$ is even. Then, for all rational x,

$$P(x,0) \implies f(x) = \max(f(x), b) \qquad\qquad \implies f(x) \geq b,$$
$$P(x,x) \implies f(2x) + b = 2f(x) \qquad\qquad \implies f(2x) = 2f(x) - b,$$
$$P(2x,x) \implies f(3x) + f(x) = 2(2f(x) - b) \qquad \implies f(3x) = 3f(x) - 2b,$$
$$P(3x,x) \implies f(4x) + 2f(x) - b = 2(3f(x) - 2b) \quad \implies f(4x) = 4f(x) - 3b.$$

Then induction gives $f(nx) = nf(x) - (n-1)b$. Therefore,

$$f(x) = a|x| + b, \quad \forall x \in \mathbb{Q},$$

which indeed is a solution, whatever are $a \in \mathbb{Q}^{\geq 0}$ and $b \in \mathbb{Q}$.

Problem 139. Let $f : \mathbb{Q} \to \mathbb{R}$ be a function such that for all rationals x and y,

$$f(x + y) = f(x)f(y) - f(xy) + 1.$$

Suppose that $f(] \neq f(]$ and

$$f\left(\frac{2017}{2018}\right) = \frac{a}{b},$$

where a and b are coprime integers. What is $a + b$? Verify your answer.

Solution (by pco). Let $P(x, y)$ be the given assertion. $P(0, 0)$ gives $f(0) = 1$ and $P(x, 1)$ implies $f(x + 1) = cf(x) + 1$, where $c = f(1) - 1$. This implies easily that

$$f(2) = c^2 + c + 1, \text{ and}$$
$$f(4) = c^4 + c^3 + c^2 + c + 1.$$

Then $P(2, 2)$ gives $c^4 = c^2$ and so $c \in \{-1, 0, 1\}$.

- $c = 0$ implies $f(x + 1) = f(x)$ and so $f(2017) = f(2018)$, impossible.

- $c = -1$ implies $f(1) = 0$, $f(2) = 1$, and $f(x+1) = 1 - f(x)$. Therefore, $f(x + 2) = f(x)$. But then

$$P(x, 2) \implies f(2x) = 1$$

  and so

$$f(x) = 1, \forall x \in \mathbb{Q},$$

  in contradiction with $f(2017) \neq f(2018)$.

- So $c = 1$ and $f(1) = 2$ and $f(x + 1) = f(x) + 1$ and so $f(x + n) = f(x) + n$. Then $P(x, n)$ implies

$$f(nx) - 1 = n(f(x) - 1).$$

  This immediately reduces to

$$f(x) = x + 1, \quad \forall x \in \mathbb{Q}.$$

So,

$$f\left(\frac{2017}{2018}\right) = \frac{2017}{2018} + 1 = \frac{4035}{2018}$$

and the required result is 6053.

4.4 Functions Over $\mathbb{Z}$

4.4.1 Number Theoretic Functions

Problem 141. Determine whether there exists a function $f : \mathbb{Z} \to \mathbb{N} \cup \{0\}$ such that $f(0) > 0$ and for each integer k, $f(k)$ is minimal value of $f(k - l) + f(l)$, where l ranges over all integers.

Solution (by pco). Note that the given equation

$$\min_{y \in \mathbb{Z}}(f(x - y) + f(y)) = f(x)$$

is equivalent to both

(1) $f(x + y) \leq f(x) + f(y)$ for all $x, y \in \mathbb{Z}$, and

(2) For any integer x, there exists an integer y such that $f(x) = f(x - y) + f(y)$.

Let $m = \min_{x \in \mathbb{Z}} f(x)$, so that $m \geq 0$. Also, take u such that $f(u) = m$. Using (2), we find that there exists $v \in \mathbb{Z}$ such that

$$m = f(u) = f(u - v) + f(v) \geq 2m,$$

and so $m = 0$. Define

$$A = \{x \in \mathbb{Z} \text{ such that } f(x) = 0\}.$$

Note that $0 \notin A$. Then, (1) implies

$$a, b \in A \implies a + b \in A \tag{4.18}$$

If all elements of A are positive, then (2) is wrong if we choose x to be the minimal member of A. If all elements of A are negative, then (2) is wrong if we choose x to be the maximal element of A. Therefore, $a = \min(A \cap \mathbb{N})$ and $b = -\max(A \cap \mathbb{N})$ exist. Let $u = \gcd(a, b)$. Then we know from Bézout's theorem that there exist non-negative integers m, n, p, q such that

$$ma + n(-b) = u \text{ and } pa + q(-b) = -u.$$

Then, using (4.18), we get that $u, -u \in A$ and so $u + (-u) = 0 \in A$, which is impossible. Hence, no such function exists.

Problem 142. Determine all functions $f : \mathbb{N} \to \mathbb{N}$ such that

$$\mathrm{lcm}(f(a), b) = \mathrm{lcm}(a, f(b))$$

for all natural numbers a and b.

Solution (by pco). Let $P(x, y)$ be the assertion $\mathrm{lcm}(f(x), y) = \mathrm{lcm}(x, f(y))$. Then $P(x, 1)$ implies

$$f(x) = \mathrm{lcm}(x, f(1)),$$

and hence

$$f(x) = \mathrm{lcm}(x, u), \quad \forall x \in \mathbb{N},$$

which is a valid solution for any choice of $u \in \mathbb{N}$ since

$$\mathrm{lcm}(\mathrm{lcm}(x, u), y) = \mathrm{lcm}(x, \mathrm{lcm}(y, u)) = \mathrm{lcm}(x, y, u).$$

Problem 144. Find all functions $f : \mathbb{N} \to \mathbb{N}$ such that

$$xf(x) + yf(y) | (x^2 + y^2)^{2018}$$

for all positive integers m, n.

Solution (by Kevin Ren). First, if x, y are relatively prime, then $x, f(y)$ are relatively prime. Indeed, supposing the contrary that $p \mid x, f(y)$ for a prime p, we get $p \mid xf(x) + yf(y) \mid (x^2 + y^2)^{2018}$, so $p \mid x^2 + y^2$ and $p \mid y^2$ implies $p \mid y$, contradiction. In particular, $f(1) = 1$ and for each prime p, $f(p) = p^n$ for some integer $n \geq 0$.

Next, we claim $f(p) = p$ for sufficiently large primes p. Indeed, since $f(1) = 1$ we get

$$1 + pf(p) | (1 + p^2)^{2018}.$$

Since

$$1 + pf(p) \leq (1 + p^2)^{2018} < p^{3 \cdot 2018},$$

we have $pf(p) \leq p^{6054}$, implying $f(p) \leq p^{6053}$. Now suppose $f(p) = p^n$ for some $2 \leq n \leq 6053$. Then the polynomial $1 + x^{n+1}$ does not divide $(1 + x^2)^{2018}$ (since the former has no repeated roots and $1 + x^{n+1} \nmid 1 + x^2$), so by polynomial long division and the fact that $1 + x^{n+1}$ is monic, we get $1 + p^{n+1} \mid Q(p)$, where Q is a nonzero polynomial at most degree n and with integer coefficients. Since $1 + p^{n+1}$ has higher degree than Q, the divisibility can only hold for finitely many primes p. This argument holds for all $2 \leq n \leq 6053$, so $f(p) \neq p$ for only finitely many primes p. Thus, $f(p) = p$ for sufficiently large primes $p > N$.

Finally, suppose $f(x) \neq x$ for some x. Choose a prime p with

$$p > \max(|x^2 - xf(x)|^{1009}, N)$$

and notice that $xf(x)+p^2 \mid (x^2+p^2)^{2018}$ implies $xf(x)+p^2 \mid (x^2-xf(x))^{2018}$. This is a contradiction since both sides are positive but the left-hand side is greater. Thus, $f(x) = x$ for all $x \in \mathbb{N}$.

Problem 146. Let $S = \{1, 2, \ldots, 999\}$. Consider a function $f : S \to S$, such that for any $n \in S$,

$$f^{n+f(n)+1}(n) = f^{nf(n)}(n) = n.$$

Prove that there exists $a \in S$, such that $f(a) = a$. Here $f^k(n)$ is k times composition of f with itself.

Solution (by Minjae Kwon from Seoul Science High School). Let $a_1, a_2, \ldots,$ $a_k \in S$ be defined in a way that $f(a_i) = a_{i+1}$ for $i = 1, 2, \ldots, k-1$ and $f(a_k) = a_1$. That is, we have a cycle. One can easily check that $f^r(a_j) = a_j$ holds for $r \geq 1$ if and only if $k \mid r$. Therefore, for $j = 1, 2, \ldots, k$, we have

$$k \mid a_j + f(a_j) + 1 \quad \text{and} \quad k \mid a_j f(a_j).$$

Take any prime factor p of k. Since $p \mid k \mid a_j f(a_j) = a_j a_{j+1}$ (assuming $a_{k+1} = a_1$) for all $j = 1, 2, \ldots, k$, there exists some j such that $p \mid a_j$. WLOG, assume that $p \mid a_1$. Then, since $p \mid k \mid a_1 + a_2 + 1$, we find that $p \mid a_2 + 1$. Then $p \mid a_2 a_3$ implies $p \mid a_3$ since $\gcd(a_2, a_2 + 1) = 1$. Then, $p \mid a_3 + a_4 + 1$ gives $p \mid a_4 + 1$ and since $p \mid a_4 a_5$, we find that $p \mid a_5$. We can continue this process to obtain $p \mid a_i$ if i is odd and $p \mid a_i + 1$ if i is even. Now, since

$$p \mid a_k + f(a_k) + 1 = a_k + a_1 + 1$$

and $p \mid a_1$, we get $p \mid a_k + 1$, and hence k is even.

It is clear that f is surjective. So, we can partition f into cycles, that is, to consider 999 points and draw a directed edge from n to $f(n)$ for all n, and partition them into connected components. Assume that there are no components of size 1. Then all cycles have an even number of vertices, while there are an odd number of vertices, a contradiction. So, there exists a connected component of size 1, say $\{a\}$, and thus $f(a) = a$ as desired.

Problem 151. Find all functions $f : \mathbb{N} \to \mathbb{N}$ such that for all positive integers a and b,

$$f(a) + f(b) - ab \mid af(a) + bf(b).$$

Solution (by Evan Chen). First, putting $m = n = 1$ gives $f(1) = 1$. Now, putting $m = 1$ gives $f(n) - n + 1 \mid nf(n) + 1$, or equivalently,

$$f(n) - n + 1 \mid n^2 - n + 1.$$

Putting $m = n$ gives $2f(n) - n^2 \mid 2nf(n)$, or equivalently,

$$2f(n) - n^2 \mid n^3.$$

These relations are nice for philosophical reasons because they imply $f(n)$ has finitely many possible values for any n. Now, the relation involving n^3 is especially nice when n is a prime, and in fact we claim that:

Claim. For $p \geq 100$ a prime, we have $f(p) = p^2$.

Proof: From $2f(p) - p^2 \mid p^3$, we have that $f(p)$ is an element of

$$\left\{ \frac{-p^3 + p^2}{2}, \frac{-p^2 + p^2}{2}, \frac{-p + p^2}{2}, \frac{-1 + p^2}{2}, \frac{1 + p^2}{2}, \frac{p + p^2}{2}, \frac{p^2 + p^2}{2}, \frac{p^3 + p^2}{2} \right\}.$$

Of these, the first two are negative hence impossible, and $f(p) = p^2$ is what we want. So we wish to exclude the other five cases. On the other hand, we know that

$$2f(p) + 2p - 2 \mid 2p^2 - 2p + 2$$

and so we can just manually check the five cases by hand (each in a routine way). The proof is complete.

Once we have arbitrarily large primes, we are happy. Fix any n. Letting m be a prime gives

$$p^2 + f(n) - pn \mid p^3 + nf(n) \iff p^2 + f(n) - pn \mid p^3 - np^2 + pn^2.$$

By considering only $p > f(n)$ we may drop the factor of p on the right, so

$$p^2 + f(n) - pn \mid p^2 - np + n^2 \iff p^2 + f(n) - pn \mid n^2 - f(n).$$

By taking p large, we conclude $f(n) = n^2$ for all positive integers n.

Problem 155. Find all functions $f : \mathbb{N} \to \mathbb{N}$ such that for all $m, n \in \mathbb{N}$ we have $f(mn) = f(m)f(n)$ and $m + n \mid f(m) + f(n)$.

Solution (by Stefan Tudose). Note that $f(x) = x^{2k+1}$ with fixed $k \in \mathbb{N} \cup \{0\}$ respects the hypothesis; we'll prove that this is the only type of function.

As $f(1) = f(1)^2$, we get $f(1) = 1$. Note that

$$p \mid f(2) f\left(\frac{p-1}{2} \right) + 1$$

for any odd prime p, so there is no odd prime p dividing $f(2)$. Obviously, $f(2) \neq 1$ as $2 + 2$ does not divide $1 + 1$, thereby $f(2) = 2^\alpha$. Inductively, $f(2^k) = 2^{k\alpha}$. As $2 + 4 | 2^\alpha + 4^\alpha$, we get that α is odd.

Fix $n \in \mathbb{N}$. Then $n + 2^k | f(n) + 2^{k\alpha}$ for any $k \geq 1$. But $n + 2^k | n^\alpha + 2^{k\alpha}$, hence $n + 2^k | f(n) - n^\alpha$. This happens for any $k \geq 1$, hence $f(n) = n^\alpha$.

4.4.2   Functions on $\mathbb{Z}^+$

Problem 156. Find all functions $f : \mathbb{N} \to \mathbb{N}$ such that

$$f(m^2 + f(n)) = f(m)^2 + n$$

for all $m, n \in \mathbb{N}$.

Solution (by pco). Let $P(x, y)$ be the assertion

$$f(x^2 + f(y)) = f(x)^2 + y.$$

Then,

$$P(z, x^2 + f(y)) \implies f(y + z^2 + f(x)^2) = f(y) + x^2 + f(z)^2.$$

Simple induction implies then

$$f(y + k(z^2 + f(x)^2)) = f(y) + k(x^2 + f(z)^2).$$

Setting $k = u^2 + f(v)^2$, we get

$$f(y + (u^2 + f(v)^2)(z^2 + f(x)^2)) = f(y) + (u^2 + f(v)^2)(x^2 + f(z)^2).$$

Swapping (u, z) and (v, x) and comparing, we get

$$(u^2 + f(v)^2)(x^2 + f(z)^2) = (z^2 + f(x)^2)(v^2 + f(u)^2).$$

Setting $u = v$, this implies $f(x)^2 = x^2 + a$ for some $a \in \mathbb{Z}$. In order for LHS to always be a perfect square, we need $a = 0$. Therefore,

$$f(x) = x, \quad \forall x \in \mathbb{N},$$

which indeed is a solution.

Problem 157. Find all functions $f : \mathbb{N} \to \mathbb{N}$ such tat $f(1) > 0$ and

$$f(m^2 + n^2) = f(m)^2 + f(n)^2$$

holds for all $m, n \in \mathbb{N} \cup \{0\}$.

Solution (by pco). Let $P(m,n)$ be the assertion $f(m^2+n^2) = f(m)^2+f(n)^2$ and let $a = f(3)$. Subtracting $P(2n-1, n+2)$ from $P(2n+1, n-2)$, we get the assertion $O(n)$ as

$$f(2n+1)^2 = f(2n-1)^2 + f(n+2)^2 - f(n-2)^2, \quad \forall n \geq 2.$$

Subtracting $P(2n-2, n+4)$ from $P(2n+2, n-4)$, we get the assertion $E(n)$ as

$$f(2n+2)^2 = f(2n-2)^2 + f(n+4)^2 - f(n-4)^2, \quad \forall n \geq 4.$$

Use $P(0,0)$, $P(1,0)$, $P(1,1)$, $P(2,0)$, and $P(2,2)$ to imply $f(0) = 0$, $f(1) = 1$, $f(2) = 2$, $f(4) = 4$, and $f(8) = 8$, respectively. Now,

$$O(2) \implies f(5)^2 = a^2 + 16 \implies (f(5), a) \in \{(4,0), (5,3)\},$$

and

$$O(3) \implies f(7)^2 = 2f(5)^2 - 1 \implies f(5) \neq 4.$$

This gives us $f(3) = 3$, $f(5) = 5$, and $f(7) = 7$. Furthermore, $P(3,0)$ implies $f(9) = 9$ and $O(4)$ implies $f(6) = 6$. We have thus prove that

$$f(n) = n, \quad \forall n \in \{0, 1, 2, 3, 4, 5, 6, 7, 8, 9\}.$$

From there, $O(n)$ and $E(n)$ easily allows us to use induction to show that $f(n) = n$ for all $n \geq 0$.

Problem 159 (*CIP alert*). Find all functions $f : \mathbb{N} \to \mathbb{R}$ such that

$$f(n) = f(n^2 + n + 1)$$

for any $n \in \mathbb{N}$.

Solution (by pco). Let $g(n) = n^2 + n + 1$ injection from $\mathbb{N}$ to $\mathbb{N}$. Let $\sim$ the equivalence relation defined over $\mathbb{N}$ as:

$$x \sim y \iff \text{ there exists } k \in \mathbb{Z}^{\geq 0} \text{ such that } \max(x, y) = g^k(\min(x, y)),$$

where g^k is the composition of g with itself k times. Note that the fact this is an equivalence relation is not immediate concerning transitivity.

Let $r : \mathbb{N} \to \mathbb{N}$ be any function which associates to a natural number a representative (unique per class) of its equivalence class. Let $h : \mathbb{N} \to \mathbb{N}$ be an arbitrary function. Then $f(x) = h(r(x))$.

This is clearly a general solution and this is a trivial expression. One certainly would be interested in a clever general representation of equivalence classes.

Problem 162. Find all functions $f : \mathbb{N} \to \mathbb{N}$ such that $f(1) = 1$ and

$$f(a + b + ab) = a + b + f(ab)$$

for all positive integerts a and b.

Solution (by pco). Let $P(x, y)$ be the assertion

$$f(xy + x + y) = f(xy) + x + y$$

for all positive integers a and b. Let $a = f(2)$. Take any $n \in \mathbb{Z}^{\geq 0}$ and $x \in \mathbb{N}$. Then, $P(2x + 1, 2^n)$ gives

$$f(2^{n+1}x + 2^{n+1} + 2x + 1) = f(2^n(2x + 1)) + 2^n + 2x + 1, \qquad (4.19)$$

and $P(2^n x + 2^n + x, 1)$ implies

$$f(2^{n+1}x + 2^{n+1} + 2x + 1) = f(2^n x + 2^n + x) + 2^n x + 2^n + x + 1. \quad (4.20)$$

Finally, we have by $P(x, 2^n)$ that

$$f(2^n x + 2^n + x) = f(2^n x) + 2^n + x. \qquad (4.21)$$

Add (4.20) and (4.21), and then subtract (4.19) to find the new assertion $Q(n, x)$ as

$$f(2^n(2x + 1)) = f(2^n x) + 2^n x + 2^n,$$

true for all $n \in \mathbb{Z}^{\geq 0}$ and $x \in \mathbb{N}$. Now take $n \geq 2$.

$$P(2, 2^n) \implies f(3 \times 2^n + 2) = f(2^{n+1}) + 2^n + 2, \qquad (4.22)$$

$$Q(1, 3 \times 2^{n-2}) \implies f(3 \times 2^n + 2) = f(3 \times 2^{n-1}) + 3 \times 2^{n-1} + 2, \quad (4.23)$$

$$Q(n - 1, 1) \implies f(3 \times 2^{n-1}) = f(2^{n-1}) + 2^n.. \qquad (4.24)$$

Now add (4.23) and (4.24) and subtract (4.22) from the result to get

$$f(2^{n+1}) = f(2^{n-1}) + 3 \times 2^{n-1},$$

and so

$$f(2^{2n}) = 2^{2n} + f(4) - 4, \quad \forall n \in \mathbb{N},$$

and

$$f(2^{2n+1}) = 2^{2n+1} + a - 2, \quad \forall n \in \mathbb{Z}^{\geq 0}.$$

Then $P(2, 2)$ implies $f(4) = a + 2$ and so

$$f(2^n) = 2^n + a - 2, \quad \forall n \in \mathbb{N}.$$

Using then $Q(n, x)$, we get

$$f(2^n(2x+1)) = f(2^n x) + 2^n x + 2^n,$$

and it is easy to get with induction that

$$f(2^n - 1) = 2^n - 1, \quad \forall n \in \mathbb{N}.$$

Hence, $f(x) = x + a - 2$. Then $P(3, 5)$ gives $a = 2$ and so

$$f(x) = x \quad \forall x \in \mathbb{N},$$

which indeed is a solution.

4.4.3   Trigonometric and Periodic Functions

Problem 163. Functions $f, g : \mathbb{Z} \to \mathbb{Z}$ satisfy

$$f(g(x) + y) = g(f(y) + x)$$

for any integers x, y. If f is bounded, prove that g is periodic.

Solution (by Evan Chen). By fixing y and varying x, we see that the image of g is contained in the image of f. Similarly, the image of f is contained in the image of g. So let us denote by S the common image of the two functions.

We color each $x \in \mathbb{Z}$ one of $|S|$ colors according to the value of $g(x)$; our aim is to show this coloring is periodic. Fix an element $N \in S$ and assume $N > 0$ (since the case $N < 0$ is analogous, and if $S = \{0\}$ there is nothing to prove).

We will only need to remember the following combinatorial information:
Claim. If p and q are the same color, then $p + N$ and $q + N$ are the same color.
Proof: We have

$$f(g(x) + p) = g(f(p) + x) = g(f(q) + x) = f(g(x) + q),$$

and $g(x)$ may take any value in S. The proof is complete.

Indeed, it's enough to show the coloring is periodic on $N\mathbb{Z} + i$, for $i = 0, 1, \ldots, N$; since then the entire coloring will have period at most

$$N \cdot \text{lcm}(P_0, \ldots, P_{n-1}),$$

where P_i was the period on $N\mathbb{Z} + i$. It is enough to show this for the $i = 0$ case by shifting. Suppose aN and bN are the same color. Then $(a + 1)N$ and $(b + 1)N$ are the same color, and so on; an easy induction now shows the coloring is periodic mod $b - a$. Since there are finitely many colors, there is some color whose elements are arbitrarily negative and that is enough to imply the result.

Remark. Let $t \colon \mathbb{Z} \to \mathbb{Z}$ be any 2017-periodic function such that $t(n) \equiv n$ (mod 2017). Then $f(x) = t(x + 13)$ and $g(x) = t(x + 37)$ is an example of a solution.

4.4.4 Inequalities

Problem 164. How many functions

$$f \colon \{1, 2, 3, \ldots, n\} \to \{1, 2, 3, \ldots, n\}$$

can be defined such that $f(1) < f(2) < f(3)$?

Solution (by scrabbler94 and pco). Here are two solutions:

1. There are $\binom{n}{3}$ ways to choose values for $f(1)$, $f(2)$, and $f(3)$. There are also n^{n-3} ways to choose values for $f(4), f(5), \ldots, f(n)$. Multiplying gives the answer $n^{n-2}(n-1)(n-2)/6$.

2. The number of possibilities for $(f(1), f(2), f(3))$ is

$$\sum_{i=1}^{n-2}\sum_{j=i+1}^{n-1}\sum_{k=j+1}^{n} 1 = \sum_{i=1}^{n-2}\sum_{j=i+1}^{n-1} (n - j)$$

$$= \sum_{i=1}^{n-2} \frac{(n-i)(n-i-1)}{2}$$

$$= \sum_{i=1}^{n-2} \frac{i^2 + i}{2}$$

$$= \frac{n(n-1)(n-2)}{6}.$$

Hence, the answer is

$$\frac{n^{n-2}(n-1)(n-2)}{6}.$$

Problem 168. Determine the number of increasing functions

$$f : (1, 2, \ldots, m) \to (1, 2, \ldots, m)$$

for which $|f(x) - f(y)| \leq |x - y|$, where $m \in \mathbb{N}$.

Solution (by pco). Enough to consider as constraint

$$f(n + 1) \in \{f(n), f(n) + 1\} \cap \{1, 2, \ldots, m\}.$$

So, a function is fully defined by positionning at most $m - f(1)$ increasing steps $+1$ in $m - 1$ positions. Hence, the requested number is

$$\sum_{i=1}^{m} \sum_{j=0}^{m-i} \binom{m-1}{j}.$$

This can be easily calculated as

$$\sum_{i=1}^{m} i \binom{m-1}{i-1} = (m + 1)2^{m-2}.$$

Problem 169. Find all surjective functions $f : \mathbb{N} \to \mathbb{N}$ such that $f(n) \geq n + (-1)^n$ holds for all $n \in \mathbb{N}$.

Solution (by pco). Let S_n be the set of natural numbers solutions of the equation $x + (-1)^x \leq n$. Obviously, this set is the set of all even numbers $\leq n - 1$ and all odd numbers $\leq n + 1$, and so

$$S_{2p} = \{1, 2, 3, \ldots, 2p - 1, 2p + 1\},$$
$$S_{2p+1} = \{1, 2, 3, \ldots, 2p + 1\}.$$

Hence, $S_1 = \{1\}$ and so $f(1) = 1$. We clearly have

$$f^{-1}([1, n]) \subseteq \bigcup_{k \in [1,n]} S_k,$$

and so,

$$f^{-1}([1, 2p]) \subseteq \{1, 2, 3, \ldots, 2p - 1, 2p + 1\},$$

and

$$f^{-1}([1, 2p + 1]) \subseteq \{1, 2, 3, \ldots, 2p + 1\}.$$

This means that $|f^{-1}([1, n])| = n$ and this implies that

$$f^{-1}(\{n\}) = f^{-1}([1, n]) \setminus f^{-1}([1, n - 1]).$$

Therefore, the unique solution is given by $f(1) = 1$, $f(2p) = 2p + 1$, and $f(2p + 1) = 2p$ for all $p \geq 1$.

4.4.5   Miscellaneous

Substitutions

Problem 172. Find all functions $f : \mathbb{Z} \to \mathbb{Z}$ satisfying

$$f(x + f(y)) = f(x)$$

for all integers x, y.

Solution (by pco). Define

$$A = \{a \in \mathbb{Z} : f(x + a) = f(x), \quad \forall x \in \mathbb{Z}\}.$$

Obviously, A is an additive subgroup of $\mathbb{Z}$ and so is equal to either $\{0\}$ or $k\mathbb{Z}$ for some $k \in \mathbb{N}$.

- If $A = \{0\}$, since $f(x) \in A$ for all x, we get the solution

$$f(x) = 0, \quad \forall x \in \mathbb{Z}.$$

- If $A = k\mathbb{Z}$ for some $k \in \mathbb{N}$, we get $f(x + k) = f(x)$ and $f(x) \equiv 0$ (mod k) for all integers x. Therefore, the solution in this case is

$$f(x) = kg\left(x - k\left\lfloor \frac{x}{k} \right\rfloor\right), \quad \forall x \in \mathbb{Z},$$

  where $g : \mathbb{Z} \to \mathbb{Z}$ is any function and k is any positive integer.

Problem 173. Find the smallest positive integer k for which there exists a colouring of the positive integers $\mathbb{N}$ with k colours and a function $f : \mathbb{N} \to \mathbb{N}$ with the following two properties:

(i) For all positive integers m, n of the same colour, $f(m + n) = f(m) + f(n)$.

(ii) There are positive integers m, n such that $f(m + n) \neq f(m) + f(n)$.

Note. In a colouring of $\mathbb{N}$ with k colours, every integer is coloured in exactly one of the k colours. In both (i) and (ii) the positive integers m, n are not necessarily distinct.

Solution (by Evan Chen). Answer: $k = 3$.
    Construction: let

$$f(n) = \begin{cases} n/3, & \text{if } n \equiv 0 \pmod 3, \\ n, & \text{otherwise.} \end{cases}$$

and color the integers modulo 3. Now we prove that for $k = 2$ such a function f must be linear, even if $f : \mathbb{N} \to \mathbb{R}^{>0}$. Call the colors blue/red and, WLOG, assume $f(1) = 1$. First, we obviously have $f(2n) = 2f(n)$ for every n.

Now we proceed by induction in the following way. Assume that $f(1) = 1$, $f(2) = 2$, ..., $f(2n) = 2n$. For brevity let $m = 2n+1$ be red and assume for contradiction that $f(m) \neq m$.

The proof now proceeds in four steps. First:

- The number $m-2$ must be blue. Indeed if $m-2$ was red we would have $f(2m-2) = f(m) + f(m-2)$ which is a contradiction as $f(2m-2) = 2f(m-1) = 2m-2$ and $f(m-2) = m-2$.

- The number 2 must be red. Indeed if it was blue then $f(m) = f(2) + f(m-2) = m$.

Observe then that $f(m+2) = f(m) + 2$ since m and 2 are both red. Now we consider two cases:

-

- If $m+2$ is red, then $f(2m+2) = f(m+2) + f(m) = (f(m)+2)+f(m)$. But $2m+2 \equiv 0 \pmod 4$ implies $f(2m+2) = f(4n+4) = 4f(n+1) = 2m+2$, contradiction.

- If $m+2$ is blue, then $2f(m) = f(2m) = f(m+2) + f(m-2) = f(m) + 2 + (m-2)$. So then $f(m) = m$ again a contradiction.

So $f(m) = m$, which completes the induction.

Problem 174. Let $n > 1$ be an integer and suppose that $a_1, a_2, \ldots, a_n$ is a sequence of n natural integers. Define the sequence $\{b_i\}$ by

$$b_1 = \left\lfloor \frac{a_2 + \cdots + a_n}{n-1} \right\rfloor,$$

$$b_i = \left\lfloor \frac{a_1 + \cdots + a_{i-1} + a_{i+1} + \cdots + a_n}{n-1} \right\rfloor, \quad \text{for} \quad i = 2, \ldots, n-1,$$

$$b_n = \left\lfloor \frac{a_1 + \cdots + a_{n-1}}{n-1} \right\rfloor.$$

Define a mapping f by

$$f(a_1, a_2, \ldots a_n) = (b_1, b_2, \ldots, b_n).$$

a) Let $g : \mathbb{N} \to \mathbb{N}$ be a function such that $g(1)$ is the number of different elements in $f(a_1, a_2, \cdots a_n)$ and $g(m)$ is the number od different elements in

$$f^m(a_1, a_2, \cdots a_n) = f(f^{m-1}(a_1, a_2, \cdots a_n)), \quad m > 1.$$

Prove that there exists $k_0 \in \mathbb{N}$ such that for $m \geq k_0$, the function $g(m)$ is periodic.

b) Prove that

$$\sum_{m=1}^{k} \frac{g(m)}{m(m+1)} < C, \quad \text{for all } k \in \mathbb{N},$$

where C is a function that doesn't depend on k.

Solution (by Nikola Velov). Note that

$$b_1 + b_2 + \cdots + b_n \leq \frac{1}{n-1} \cdot ((n-1)a_1 + (n-1)a_2 + \cdots + (n-1)a_n) = a_1 + a_2 + \cdots + a_n.$$

This means that the sum of the elements of the sequence is a monovariant. Because the sum of the elements is a natural number, it will reach a minimum number k after a finite number of steps. Afterwards, after every step the sum stays the same because it is non-increasing, and the minimum is already reached. Because the number of different solutions of

$$x_1 + x_2 + \cdots + x_n = k$$

in positive integers is finite, after a finite number of moves after k is reached we will get the same sequence of elements by Pigeonhole principle. This proves that $g(m)$ is periodic.

Now for the second part, it's easy to see that g being periodic after a fixed k_0 implies that it takes only finitely many values, so there is a constant C such that $g(n) < C$ for all $n \in \mathbb{N}$. Now we have

$$\sum_{m=1}^{k} \frac{g(m)}{m(m+1)} < C \cdot \sum_{m=1}^{k} \frac{1}{m(m+1)}$$

$$= C \cdot \sum_{m=1}^{k} \left(\frac{1}{m} - \frac{1}{m+1} \right)$$

$$= C \cdot \left(1 - \frac{1}{k+1} \right) < C.$$

We are done.

Problem 175. Find all functions $f : \mathbb{N} \to \mathbb{N} \cup \{0\}$ such that $f(f(n)) = f(n+1) - f(n)$ for all positive integers n.

Solution (by pco). Let $P(n)$ be the assertion

$$f(f(n)) = f(n+1) - f(n).$$

Note that this equation implies $f(n) > 0$ for all $n > 0$, else LHS is not defined. As a consequence, the above equation implies $f(n+1) > f(n)$ and so f is strictly increasing. Adding $P(1), P(2), \ldots, P(n)$, we get

$$\sum_{k=1}^{n} f(f(k)) = f(n+1) - f(1).$$

Suppose there exists $m > 0$ such that $f(m) > m$. Setting then in above equality $n = f(m) - 1$, we get

$$\sum_{k=1}^{f(m)-1} f(f(k)) = f(f(m)) - f(1).$$

Since $m \leq f(m) - 1$, this is

$$f(1) + \sum_{k=1, k\neq m}^{f(m)-1} f(f(k)) = 0.$$

Therefore, all summands in LHS are equal to zero, which is impossible. Hence, $f(m) \leq m$ and so, since f is strictly increasing, we must have $f(n) = n$ for all $n > 0$, which unfortunately is not a solution.

Appendices

Appendix A

Hints and Final Answers

Problem 3 (by pco). Let $P(x, y, z)$ be the given assertion. Prove that $f(0) = 0$. Use $P\left(x, \frac{x^2}{1-f(1)}, 1\right)$ to show that $f(1) = 1$. Then show that f is odd and find the additive Cauchy.

Problem 4. Answer: no such function exists. Try to show that f is a bijection.

Problem 5 (by Tuzson Zoltán). Do the change of variables $y \to -y$ to find that f is odd. Then define $g(x + y) = f(x + y)/(f(x) + f(y))$ and imply that g is a constant function. Then it turns into the classical Cauchy.

Problem 6. Define $g(x) = f(x)/x^a$ and $h(x) = g(e^x)$ and imply that $h(x) = kx$ for some k.

Problem 7. First show that $f(1) = 1$ and then $f(f(t)) = t$. This transforms the given equation into a multilicative Cauchy form. Fill in the details!

Problem 9. The solutions are $f \equiv 0$ and $f(x) = \pm e^{cx^2}$.

Problem 10. The solutions are $f(x) = 0$ and $f(x) = x + a$ for any real a.

Problem 11. Use $P(f(x), x)$ and $P(x, u)$, wherer P is the given assertion and u is such that $f(u) = 0$ to get $f(0) = 0$. You will reach the classic additive Cauchy.

Problem 12. Kronecker's theorem.

Problem 13. The general solution is $f(x) = ax + b$ for any real a, b. WLOG, assume $f(0) = 0$. Let $a, b > 0$ and define the sequences $\{x_n\}$ and $\{y_n\}$ recursively so that $x_1 = a$ and $y_1 = b$ and

$$x_{n+1} = \frac{x_n}{y_n + 1} \quad \text{and} \quad y_{n+1} = \frac{(x_n + y_n + 1)y_n}{y_n + 1}$$

for all $n \geq 1$. Then discover Cauchy's classical.

Problem 14 (by pco). For the first part: show with induction that for all $x \in \mathbb{R}$ and all integers $n \geq 0$,

$$f\left(2f(x) - x + \frac{x - f(x)}{2^{n-1}}\right) = 2f(x) - x + \frac{x - f(x)}{2^n}.$$

Then set $n \to \infty$.

Problem 15 (by MSTang). If the given assertion is supposed to be $P(x, y)$, calculate $P(y, x)$ and choose y to be a constant times x (find the appropriate constant).

Problem 17 (by pco).   1. The only injective Patrician function is $f(x) = x + 1$.

2. The only surjective Patrician function is $f(x) = x + 1$.

3. Let $\mathbb{Q}$ and A be two supplementary sub-vectorspaces of the $\mathbb{Q}$-vectorspace $\mathbb{R}$. Let $q : \mathbb{R} \to \mathbb{Q}$ and $a : \mathbb{R} \to A$ be the projections of a real x in $(\mathbb{Q}, A)$. Then choose $f(x) = q(x) + 1$.

Problem 19. Take the derivative.

Problem 20. The only solutions are $f(x) = \pm x$.

Problem 22. The function $f(x) = 2x$ is the unique solution. Use $P(f(y) - 2y, y)$ to find that for all $y \in \mathbb{R}$, either $f(y) = 2y$ or $f(f(y) - 2y) = 0$.

Problem 23 (by pco). Show that f is injective. Break the problem into 2 cases: $f(0) = 0$, which gives $f \equiv 0$, and $f(0) \neq 0$, in which case $f(2) = 1$. Show in the latter case, using $P(x, 1)$, that $f(x) = x - 1$ is the only solution.

Problem 24. $f(x) = g(x) = x$ is the only solution.

Problem 25. Show that f is surjective. Then find $f(0)$ and for each $x \in \mathbb{R}$, take z to be the number such that $f(z) = x + f(x)$. Show then that $z = 0$.

Problem 26. The answer is $f(x) = ax + b$ for any real b. Prove that f is a surjection first. Then, show that it is periodic and imply injectivity.

Problem 30. Prove that if $f(x) < 1$, then we have $x < 1$. Show that f is injective and then prove that $f(x) = x$ for all x in the domain.

Problem 31. Prove that the given equation implies $yz + e^y xz = xz + e^x yz$.

Problem 32. Choose $f(n) = a(1 + (-1)^n) + \frac{1 - (-1)^n}{2}$.

Problem 34. The given statement is true.

Problem 35. Use $P(x/2, x/2)$ and $P(x, 2a - x)$ to obtain an upper bound for $f(x)$ on the interval $(0, a]$ for any real $a > 0$. Define $\{x_n\}$ as $x_0 = 1$ and $x_{n+1} = x_n + \frac{2}{f(x_n)}$. Use $P(x_n, 2/f(x_n))$ to show that $f(x_n) > 2^n u$ and then show that $f(x)$ is not upper bounded in the interval $(0, 1 + 4/u]$.

Problem 37 (by pco). The general solution is

$$f(x) = (-1)^{\lfloor \frac{x}{27} \rfloor} g(\{\frac{x}{27}\}),$$

where $g : [0, 1) \to \mathbb{R}$ is an arbitrary function.

Problem 39. The answer is $f(x) = ax + b$ for any real b. Prove that f is a surjection first. Then, show that it is periodic and imply injectivity.

Problem 43. Show that if $p(x + y) = \sum a_{ij} x^i y^j$, then there exists an even positive i such that $a_{ij} \neq 0$. Prove that f is linear. Find the solutions

- $c = 0$ implies the solution

$$f(x) = 0, \quad \forall x \in \mathbb{R},$$

which indeed is a solution if $p(0) = 0$.

- $c = 1$ implies the solution

$$f(x) = x, \quad \forall x \in \mathbb{R},$$

which indeed is a solution.

- $c = -1$ implies the solution

$$f(x) = -x, \quad \forall x \in \mathbb{R},$$

which indeed is a solution if $p(x)$ is an odd polynomial.

Problem 45. Prove that 1) $f(x) \geq x$ and $g(x) \geq x$, 2) If $f(x+a) = f(x)+b$ for all $x > 0$, then $a = b$, and 3) $g(x) - f(x)$ is constant.

Problem 46 (by pco). Prove the following:

1. If $f(x + a) = f(x) + b \; \forall x > 0$ for some $a, b > 0$, then $a = b$.

2. $f(x) = x$ for any $x > 0$.

3. $g(x) = x$ for all $x > 0$.

Problem 47. The only solution is $f(x) = 2x$.

Problem 48. The only solution is $f(x) = x + c$ whatever is $c \geq 0$.

Problem 49. The only solution is $f(x) = g(x) = 1/\sqrt{2}$.

Problem 51. Use substitutions $P(x + f(z), y), P(x, z)$, and $P(x + y, z)$ to get a new assertion. Then swap y and z to prove that the solutions are $f(x) = x + a$ for any $a \geq 0$.

Problem 56 (by babu2001). The only solution is $f \equiv 3$. Compare $P(x, y, z)$ and $P(xy, 1, z)$.

Problem 57. Set $f(1 + f(1)) = C$. Then,

$$f(x) = \left(\frac{(C+1)f(1 + f(\frac{1}{C+1}))}{C} - 1 \right) x, \quad \forall x > 0.$$

Problem 61. No such function exists. Try computing $P(1, x+y-1)$, where $P(\cdot, \cdot)$ is the given assertion.

Problem 62. Define $g(x)$ such that $g(x) = 1/f(x)$. Then, show that g is linear and $f(x) = 1/g(x) = 1/(mx + c)$ for all $x \in \mathbb{R}^+$.

Problem 64 (by pco). Let $u = 1 + f(1)$ and prove that

$$\frac{3}{4}x - \frac{u}{2} < f(x) < \frac{3}{2}x + \frac{u}{2}.$$

Then if $a_n x - b_n u < f(x) < c_n x + d_n u$ for all $x > 0$, then

$$(a_1, b_1, c_1, d_1) = \left(\frac{3}{4}, \frac{1}{2}, \frac{3}{2}, \frac{1}{2} \right), \quad \text{and}$$

$$(a_{n+1}, b_{n+1}, c_{n+1}, d_{n+1}) = \left(\frac{3 - c_n}{2}, \frac{c_n + d_n - 1}{2}, \frac{3 - a_n}{2}, \frac{-a_n + b_n + 1}{2} \right)$$

and so (a_n, b_n, c_n, d_n) is convergent towards $(1, 0, 1, 0)$. This confirms that the only solution is $f(x) = x$.

Problem 71 (by pco). Easy induction gives

$$f\left(x + \sum_{i=1}^{n} y_i^2 \right) \geq f(x) + \sum_{i=1}^{n} y_i$$

for all x and y_i such that $x, x + \sum_{i=1}^{n} y_i^2 \in [0, 2017]$. Choose then $x = 0$ and $y_i = 1/\sqrt{n}$ for all i, and this becomes

$$f(1) \geq f(0) + \sqrt{n}$$

for all positive integers n. This is impossible.

Problem 72 (by DerJan).

1. Show that $f(0) = 0$ and $f(x) \leq x$ and conclude that $f(-1) = -1$.

2. Use $P(x+1, -1)$ and $P(1, x)$ to imply $f(x) \geq x$.

Problem 74. The solutions are of the form $f(x) = ax + b$, where $a, b \in \mathbb{R}$ and $a \geq 0$.

Problem 76 (by pco). This is the Cantor function. So,

$$f\left(\frac{5}{8}\right) = f((\overline{0.1\ldots})_3) = (\overline{0.1})_2 = \frac{1}{2}.$$

Problem 77 (by pco). Define $g(x) = f(1/x)$, $h(x) = xg(x) - 1/2$, and $k(x) = h(x+1/2)$ and show that $k(-x) = -k(x)$ in the appropriate interval.

Problem 83. The only solution is $f(x) = x^2 + 3$.

Problem 85 (by pco). Let $a = f(0)$.

- If $a = 0$, the only solution is $f \equiv 0$.

- If $a > 0$, then f is injective and the only solution is $f(x) = x + 1$ for all $x \in \mathbb{R}$.

- If $a < 0$, the only solution is $f(x) = -x - 1$ for all $x \in \mathbb{R}$.

Problem 86. Show that $f(x) = \pm x/\alpha$ and imply, using $f(f(x)^2) = x^2$, that $\alpha = \pm 1$. If $\alpha \neq -1$, there is no solution, and you should be able to guess the solution for $\alpha = -1$.

Problem 88. The answer is:

$$g(t) = \begin{cases} 1, & \text{if } t < 0, \\ 2, & \text{if } t = 0, \\ 3, & \text{if } 0 < t < \frac{4}{27}, \\ 2, & \text{if } t = \frac{4}{27}, \\ 1, & \text{if } t > \frac{4}{27}. \end{cases}$$

Problem 89. The answer is $f(x,y) = x^2 y$.

Problem 93 (by pco). Yes, there exist infinitely many such functions. Write

$$f(x) = g(x + \frac{1}{2}) - \frac{1}{2}$$

and the equation becomes

$$g(g(x)) = x^2 + \frac{13}{4}.$$

It is easy to build such a function piece per piece over $\mathbb{R}^{\geq 0}$ and to extend aver $\mathbb{R}^-$ by symmetry.

Problem 95 (taken from website matol.kz). Try to prove that

$$(x + y^2)f(yf(x)) = xyf(y^2 + f(x)),$$

and

$$(x + y^2)\left(f(yf(x)) + f(-yf(x))\right) = 0.$$

Then consider the set of all values of t for which $f(t) = 0$. Consider three cases for this set to obtain the three solutions:

- $f(x) = x$ for all real x.

- $f \equiv 0$.

-
$$f(x) = \begin{cases} 0, & \text{if } x \neq -a^2, \\ a, & \text{if } x = -a^2. \end{cases}$$

where a is any real number with $a \in (-\infty, -1] \cup (0, +\infty)$.

Problem 96. The only solutions are $f \equiv 0$ and $f(x) = x^2$ for all x.

Problem 98. Consider $P(y, x)$ (the given assertion is supposed to be $P(x, y)$) and apply f on the obtained equation.

Problem 102 (by pco). Show that $f(x) > 1$ holds for all $x > 0$.Then show that there are no injective solutions. Finally, show that the only non-injective solution is $f(x) = 2$ for all $x > 0$.

Problem 103. The all-zero function is the trivial solution. The non-trivial solutions are $f(x) = x$, $f(x) = -x$, and $f(x) = |x|$ for all real x.

Problem 105. The non-trivial solution is $f(x) = x - x^2$.

Problem 108. The solutions are $f \equiv 0$ and $f(x) = \pm x$.

Problem 109. Suppose that there exists u such that $f(u) = 0$. Then play with $P(-u, 2u)$.

Problem 111. The solutions are $f(x) = \lfloor x \rfloor$, and $f(x) = -\lfloor x \rfloor$.

Problem 113. Define $g(x) = f(x) - \lfloor x \rfloor$ and use the fact that

$$\lfloor x + y \rfloor - \lfloor x \rfloor - \lfloor y \rfloor = \lfloor \{x\} + \{y\} \rfloor$$

to show that g satisfies the additive Cauchy. The solutions are $f(x) = x$ and $f(x) = \lfloor x \rfloor$.

Problem 114. It should be easy to find all such functions if there is some $x \neq 0$ for which $f(x) = 0$. Otherwise, let $a = f(0)$ and $c = f(1)$ and consider $P(-c^2, c/f(-c^2))$ and $P(-c^2, c/f(-c^2))$, where $P(\cdot, \cdot)$ is the given assertion.

Problem 115. Plug in $x = 0$. The only answer is $f \equiv 0$.

Problem 118. The answer is $(f(0), g(0)) = (0, 1)$.

Problem 123. Use $P((x+y)/2, (x-y)/2)$ to find $f(x) = cx$ for all x, where $c = f(1)$.

Problem 125. $f(2017)$ is either 0 or 1.

Problem 126. Answer: the identity function and the absolute value function.

Problem 128. Calculate $P(0, y)$ and $P(x, 0)$. If $f(0) = 0$, show that $f \equiv 0$. If $f(0) \neq 0$, show that $f \equiv 1$.

Problem 129. Use $a = (x - 1)/2$, $b = (x + 1)/2$, and $c = (1 - x)/2$.

Problem 133. Define $g(x) = f(1/x)$ and prove that $g(x + y) = g(x) + g(y) - c$ for some c.

Problem 134. The key is $f(x + y) = f(x)f(y)$, and the answer is $f(x) = be^{ax} \; \forall x \in \mathbb{Q}$.

Problem 136. The only solution is

$$f\left(\frac{p}{q}\right) = k \left(\frac{q}{\gcd(p, q)}\right)^2$$

for all $p, q \in \mathbb{N}$ and any choice of $k \in \mathbb{Q}^+$.

Problem 137 (by Domingues3). $f(x)$ is the numerator of x (when x is written as a reduced fraction).

Problem 139. The only solution is $f(x) = x+1$ and so the answer is 6053.

Problem 143 (by TLP.39). There are no such functions. Show that this is equivalent to finding all functions $f, h : \mathbb{Q}^+ \to \mathbb{N}$ such that

$$\frac{\gcd\left(f(x)f(x/a),\, f(1/x)f(a/x)\right)}{\operatorname{lcm}(f(x), f(a/x))} = h(a)$$

for all $x, a \in \mathbb{Q}^+$. Let the above assertion be $P(x, a)$. Prove, using $P(k, k^2)$ and $P(x, k^2)$ that $f(a) \mid f(b)$ for all positive rationals a and b. Conclude.

Problem 144. Show that $f(1) = 1$ and $f(p) = p$ for sufficiently large primes p. Conclude that $f(x) = x$ for all $x \in \mathbb{N}$.

Problem 147 (by Aiscrim). For any odd prime p, use the fact that

$$p \mid f(2) f\left(\frac{p-1}{2}\right) + 1$$

to conclude that $f(2)$ is an odd power of 2, say $f(2) = 2^\alpha$. Then show by induction that $f(2^k) = 2^{k\alpha}$ for all k. For a fixed n, use $n + 2^k \mid f(n) + 2^{k\alpha}$ and $n + 2^k \mid n^\alpha + 2^{k\alpha}$ to finish the problem.

Problem 148. Solutions:

- $f(n) = 0, \quad \forall n \in \mathbb{N}$.

- $f(n) = 1, \quad \forall n \in \mathbb{N}$.

- $f(n) = 0, \quad \forall n \equiv 0 \pmod{2017}$ and $f(n) = 1, \quad \forall n \not\equiv 0 \pmod{2017}$.

- $f(n) = \left(\frac{n}{2017}\right), \quad \forall n \in \mathbb{N}$, where $\left(\frac{\cdot}{\cdot}\right)$ is the Legnedre's symbol.

Problem 149.

a) For $n = 2$, any prime p and integers $a = p$ and $b = p^k$ (with $k \geq 2$) works. For $n > 2$, if n is odd, use Lifting The Exponent Lemma.

b) Use the fact that $f(xy) \leq f(x) + f(y)$ for all $x, y \in \mathbb{N}$.

Problem 150. The answer is $f(x) = x^2$ for all $x \in \mathbb{N}$.

Problem 153. Use the fact that $f(d(n)) = d(f(n))$, where $d(n)$ is the number of divisors of n.

Problem 154. The answer is 12066.

Problem 155. Choose $m = p - 1$ and $n = 1$ to obtain

$$p \mid f(2) f\left(\frac{p-1}{2}\right) + 1$$

for any odd prime p.

Problem 158 (by pco). Possibly a CIP. Here for example, we have a lot of solutions and there may exist serious doubts about the existence of a general form giving all of them:

$$f(n) = 1, \quad \forall n \in \mathbb{N},$$
$$f(n) = n, \quad \forall n \in \mathbb{N},$$
$$f(n) = 2^u(1 + (-1)^n) + \frac{1 - (-1)^n}{2}, \quad \forall n \in \mathbb{N}, u \in \{0, 1, 2, \ldots, k-1\}$$
$$f(n) = 2^u(1 - (-1)^n) + \frac{1 + (-1)^n}{2}, \quad \forall n \in \mathbb{N}, u \in \{0, 1, 2, \ldots, k-1\}.$$

Problem 160. Take $g(x) = f(x) - 1$ so that $g(2x) = g(x)^2$. Then take $g(x) = e^{h(x)}$ and equation becomes $h(2x) = 2h(x)$.

Problem 161. Define $g(x) = f(x) - x^n$.

Problem 165. First prove that $f(1) = 1$. Then use $P(1, y)$ and $P(x, 1)$ to conclude that the only solution is the identity function.

Problem 170 (by GaryTam). Show that f is strictly increasing using the fact that if $x \geq y$, then $f(x) \geq y$. The only solution is the identity function.

Problem 171. Note that $f(n)$ is just swapping 0 and 1 in binary representation of n (from rightmost digit up to and including the leftmost binary 1).

Problem 175. There are no such functions.

Appendix B

Contributors

In the next few pages, there is a list of AoPS users who posted the problems in this book on AoPS. I salute all the people in this list for posting such nice questions! The list is ordered based on the appearance of the problem in the book. I have also included the dates on which the problems were posted.

I know the real names of several users in this list, but I'm not revealing the names to respect their privacy.

To see a list of contributors of the solutions, please refer to the preface of the book.

1. 2009_hy_26
   [*April 5, 2018*]

2. Samsuman
   [*April 4, 2018*]

3. Muradjl
   [*March 31, 2018*]

4. Taha1381
   [*January 13, 2018*]

5. makar
   [*January 10, 2018*]

6. Anis2017
   [*January 1, 2018*]

7. Abhinandan18
   [*November 27, 2016*]

8. Catalin
   [*April 6, 2018*]

9. mathenthusiastic
   [*April 5, 2018*]

10. ShR
    [*March 11, 2018*]

11. hakarimian
    [*January 15, 2018*]

12. Pirkuliyev Rovsen
    [*January 10, 2018*]

13. Mathuzb
    [*January 3, 2018*]

14. felix_brook
    [*August 8, 2017*]

15. Tintarn
    [*April 2, 2017*]

16. rmtf1111
    [*March 19, 2017*]

17. Hamel
    [*April 29, 2018*]

18. Mathuzb
    [*April 21, 2018*]

19. Catalin
    [*April 12, 2018*]

20. RnstTrjyn
    [*April 10, 2018*]

21. Taha1381
    [*April 3, 2018*]

22. CinarArslan
    [*March 26, 2018*]

23. kakasmino
    [*March 22, 2018*]

24. Taha1381
    [*March 20, 2018*]

25. Strong_TTM
    [*January 5, 2017*]

26. umaru
    [*October 3, 2017*]

27. YHA
    [*July 25, 2017*]

28. Borbas
    [*May 3, 2017*]

29. tenplusten
    [*January 27, 2017*]

30. socrates
    [*October 28, 2014*]

31. knm2608
    [*March 9, 2018*]

32. Xurshid.Turgunboyev
    [*January 4, 2018*]

33. Pirkuliyev Rovsen
    [*July 27, 2017*]

34. Tintarn
    [*April 2, 2017*]

35. mahanmath
    [*March 4, 2011*]

36. GeometryIsMyWeakness
    [*April 19, 2018*]

37. mathematics4u
    [*April 7, 2018*]

38. MATH1945
    [*March 30, 2018*]

39. umaru
    [*October 3, 2017*]

40. Amir Hossein
    [*May 22, 2018*]

41. Taha1381
    [*March 20, 2018*]

42. mathisreal
    [*January 12, 2018*]

43. Xurshid.Turgunboyev
    [*January 4, 2018*]

44. bgn
    [*April 24, 2017*]

45. Taha1381
    [*March 20, 2018*]

46. Taha1381
    [*March 20, 2018*]

47. Taha1381
    [*March 20, 2018*]

48. Taha1381
    [*March 20, 2018*]

49. Taha1381
    [*March 20, 2018*]

50. R8450932
    [*March 17, 2018*]

51. Mathuzb
    [*January 3, 2018*]

52. Caspper
    [*August 21, 2017*]

53. MAITHANHHUY
    [*June 17, 2017*]

54. FedeX333X
    [*June 5, 2017*]

55. socrates
    [*April 25, 2017*]

56. Duarti
    [*April 1, 2017*]

57. proximo
    [*March 31, 2017*]

58. mathwizard888
    [*July 19, 2017*]

60. socrates
    [*April 6, 2016*]

61. IstekOlympiadTeam
    [*November 2, 2015*]

62. behdad.math.math
    [*January 1, 2010*]

63. lmht
    [*April 11, 2018*]

64. Taha1381
   [March 20, 2018]

65. mathisreal
   [January 12, 2018]

66. socrates
   [May 2, 2017]

67. tenplusten
   [April 29, 2018]

68. jonny
   [April 16, 2018]

69. Xurshid.Turgunboyev
   [April 13, 2018]

70. Muradjl
   [April 1, 2018]

71. Muradjl
   [March 31, 2018]

72. OPSEC2
   [January 27, 2018]

73. rkm0959
   [November 12, 2017]

74. whatshisbucket
   [June 26, 2017]

75. Jason99
   [May 1, 2018]

76. DurdonTyler
   [May 1, 2018]

77. silvergrasshopper
   [April 28, 2018]

78. steppewolf
   [April 21, 2018]

79. jd
   [April 18, 2018]

80. Dadgarnia
   [April 15, 2018]

81. Catalin
   [April 12, 2018]

82. Mathuzb
   [December 20, 2017]

83. MMike
   [October 28, 2017]

84. hieu04092001
   [September 19, 2017]

85. ABCDE
   [July 21, 2017]

86. socrates
   [June 10, 2017]

87. Strong_TTM
   [June 3, 2017]

88. MustafaKemal
   [May 9, 2017]

89. bgn
   [April 26, 2017]

90. socrates
   [April 25, 2017]

91. djmathman
   [April 7, 2017]

92. four4th
   [March 29, 2017]

93. ALA.HGH
   [March 24, 2017]

94. Hello_Kitty
   [January 29, 2017]

95. user01
[*January 14, 2017*]

96. acegikmoqsuwy2000
[*January 3, 2017*]

97. micliva
[*October 20, 2013*]

98. Amir Hossein
[*May 22, 2018*]

99. Amir Hossein
[*May 22, 2018*]

100. abbosjon2002
[*May 1, 2018*]

101. RnstTrjyn
[*April 17, 2018*]

102. RnstTrjyn
[*April 13, 2018*]

103. Georgemoukas
[*April 12, 2018*]

104. longnhat2002
[*April 9, 2018*]

105. FieldBird
[*April 5, 2018*]

106. futurestar
[*April 5, 2018*]

107. Pirkuliyev Rovsen
[*March 30, 2018*]

108. FEcreater
[*March 10, 2018*]

109. FEcreater
[*March 10, 2018*]

110. Medjl
[*February 1, 2018*]

111. rightways
[*January 14, 2018*]

112. Taha1381
[*January 13, 2018*]

113. lminsl
[*January 7, 2018*]

114. JANMATH111
[*January 2, 2018*]

115. MF163
[*November 14, 2017*]

116. quangminhltv99
[*October 22, 2017*]

117. YanYau
[*October 21, 2017*]

118. Taha1381
[*September 2, 2017*]

119. YanYau
[*October 21, 2017*]

120. abeker
[*August 25, 2017*]

121. LittelPerel
[*August 8, 2017*]

122. ShinyDitto
[*July 18, 2017*]

123. cjquines0
[*April 13, 2017*]

124. virnoy
[*March 31, 2017*]

125. pinetree1
[*February 19, 2017*]

126. Ankoganit
[*January 17, 2017*]

127. Pirkuliyev Rovsen
[
[*January 3, 2017*]]

130. Kezer
[*October 9, 2014*]

131. Amir Hossein
[*January 28, 2010*]

132. Arne
[*August 31, 2003*]

133. Taha1381
[*January 14, 2018*]

134. wanwan4343
[*July 12, 2018*]

135. Matin Yousefi
[*April 17, 2018*]

136. JokerZ
[*March 14, 2018*]

137. socrates
[*May 6, 2017*]

138. Muradjl
[*March 31, 2018*]

139. ShantoBro
[*January 17, 2018*]

140. yaron235
[*December 22, 2016*]

141. mruczek
[*April 30, 2018*]

142. GorgonMathDota
[*April 21, 2018*]

143. Muradjl
[*Posted by on March 25, 2018*]

144. Muradjl
[*March 19, 2018*]

145. mofumofu
[*February 13, 2018*]

146. mofumofu
[*February 13, 2018*]

147. jrc1729
[*January 21, 2018*]

148. Muradjl
[*January 14, 2018*]

149. fattypiggy123
[*November 14, 2017*]

150. Snakes
[*July 19, 2017*]

151. dangerousliri
[*July 19, 2017*]

152. aleksam
[*May 21, 2017*]

153. InCtrl
[*March 31, 2017*]

154. pinetree1
[*February 19, 2017*]

155. mberke
[*April 5, 2016*]

156. Dayal83603
[*April 27, 2018*]

157. cassia
[*April 12, 2018*]

158. Muradjl
[*March 11, 2018*]

159. Alex27
     [*January 7, 2018*]

160. CinarArslan
     [*January 11, 2018*]

161. Stefan4024
     [*April 8, 2017*]

162. Cuzo
     [*April 5, 2017*]

163. mofumofu
     [*January 1, 2018*]

164. Masac9
     [*April 19, 2018*]

165. BartSimpsons
     [*December 27, 2017*]

166. rkm0959
     [*March 25, 2017*]

167. drkim
     [*January 20, 2017*]

168. Pirkuliyev Rovsen
     [*January 8, 2017*]

169. soruz
     [*January 8, 2011*]

170. dondigo
     [*February 21, 2006*]

171. Sarbajit10598
     [*March 19, 2018*]

172. SHARKYKESA
     [*December 22, 2017*]

173. IstekOlympiadTeam
     [*April 8, 2017*]

174. Stefan4024
     [*April 8, 2017*]

175. lwwwww
     [*January 17, 2017*]

Made in the USA
Middletown, DE
20 July 2024

57760691R00103